BEYOND THE JUMP SHOT

BEYOND THE JUMP SHOT

The Elevated Life of Kenny Sailors

Debbie Sorensen

Clovercroft Publishing

Beyond the Jump Shot: The Elevated Life of Kenny Sailors

Published by Clovercroft Publishing, Franklin, Tennessee
CloverCroftPublishingGroup.com

Interior Design and Cover Design by Suzanne Lawing

Cover photo courtesy of the Boston Celtics/NBA Photos

Printed in the United States of America

ISBN: 978-1-956370-53-9 (print)

Dedicated to:
Single mothers and fatherless children.

CONTENTS

INTRODUCTION

If you love basketball, you'll love this story. If you don't love basketball, you'll love this story. If you want to be inspired by a young boy who was so desperate he jumped, you'll love this story.

I'm not a basketball expert or a personal historian. Many other writers have covered those topics on Kenny Sailors. But I do love a good story. My story is about a friend who chose to make a difference in life.

Kenny Sailors discovered a way to shoot a basketball over an older and bigger brother. He became legendary throughout basketball and made history with the game-changing jump shot. To be clear, before the three-point shot impacted basketball, there was the jump shot.

I first met Kenny in the summer of 1978 when my husband and I moved to the Copper River Valley in southcentral Alaska. Neighbors Marilynne and Kenny Sailors heard we were new to the area and invited us to a potluck meal to meet folks.

On a recommendation from the Sailors, Russ and I attended the Native Chapel in nearby Gulkana Village. When a weekly Bible study started at the Sailors' home, Marilynne invited me to join them. In the winter it was not unusual for Kenny to help me shovel my Volkswagen Bug out of a pile of snow in their yard. He was a good man and, good with a shovel.

We were told that in 1943, Kenny had played on the University of Wyoming national championship basketball team in Madison Square Garden. He also played for the Boston Celtics in 1950-51, then went into politics, before switching careers to guiding and hunting.

The development of the jump shot shook up the world of basketball so much that Kenny Sailors was named, "Most Valuable Player NCAA championships," in 1943.

How could a poor, fatherless kid, raised by a single mother on a Wyoming farm, develop an unusual move and change basketball history?

I began to dig deeper into this inspiring story. Kenny Sailors not only changed a sport but changed countless lives through his willingness to become involved and make a difference.

When asked about the jump shot, the basketball veteran would simply respond, "There's no way of knowing which kid, somewhere, jumped in the air and shot a basketball. Yes, I had a jump shot. I jumped to score against my big brother."

Legendary coach of DePaul University, Ray Meyer, had something to say on the jump shot development.

"Sailors may not have been the first player to jump in the air and shoot the ball," Meyer continued. "But he developed the shot that's being used today."

"That's the way he put it," Kenny said. "And I like that."

In 1946 Eric Schaal, a photographer for *Life* magazine, captured the Wyoming Cowboys guard, suspended above the basketball court of Madison Square Garden. That picture highlighted Kenny's jump and shot throughout the world of sports. Going into the air, Sailors launched the basketball into a new dimension of play.

Between 1921 and 2016, Kenny's life covered nearly a century of stunning changes. Kenny's Mother, Cora Sailors, was a determined frontier pioneer who overcame the hardships of life with determination and grit. With her faith in God, she was an example to help her son overcome unfairness and challenges. Kenny was nearly tossed out to die by a desperate father who didn't want another mouth to feed. Soon after, Ed Sailors abandoned his family. At that point, Cora determined, she would raise her sons to become men.

Kenny became a basketball pioneer who forged his way in life. His big brother Bud, caused him to get creative as they shot basketballs toward the round iron rim, nailed to the wooden backboard, on the windmill of their Wyoming farm.

Later in high school and college, two special coaches came alongside the young man and took Kenny under their wings. Those men helped him deal with the rejection and abandonment that the trauma in his early life had created. Floyd Foreman and Everett Shelton went on to reinforce his ballhandling and leadership skills.

This innovator went on to have a family and succeed in life. He disappeared for several decades into the American wilderness while he worked his outdoor businesses. When he re-emerged, he taught high school and established a girls' basketball program in the Alaska public schools. Kenny elevated the lives of young and old alike.

I am one of the many people Kenny and Marilynne Sailors encouraged.

GLOSSARY

Before starting the book, read through this glossary. The following word definitions will be interesting and helpful.

anchor clacker—a sailor

Alaska Milepost magazine—the best-selling traveler's guide to Alaska

Alyeska—pronounced Al-YES-ka, an Aleut word, means "great land"

Athabascan—native of central and interior Alaska

Aurora Borealis—natural display of lights in the sky at high latitudes

bag an animal—harvest a wild game animal or bird

barking up the wrong tree—looking for an answer in the wrong place

barter—trade services or goods rather than paying for something

between a rock and a hard spot—in a difficult situation and a decision must be made

Boone and Crockett—record-keeping system for designating recognition to exceptional North American big-game animals.

bunch of bunk—nonsense, insincere, or empty talk

burr under his saddle—someone or something that is a constant cause of annoyance or irritation

bush pilot—a pilot who flies a small aircraft into remote areas button up—be quiet, now!

cache—(pronounced "cash") small storage building, built on stilts to be inaccessible to animals

cackleberry—chicken egg

cager—an athlete who plays basketball

CAM—an acronym for Central Alaska Mission

Caribou Clatters—radio program of KCAM Radio in Glennallen

Cayuse—small native horse

Cheechako—a newcomer to Alaska

chew the fat—converse idly, make small talk

commenced—to begin an activity with decisive action

Corn Tassel—the nickname Marilynne gave to Kenny

country bumpkin—an awkward or unsophisticated person from out of town

cracker box—a nickname in early basketball, for a smaller-than-usual gym, with much louder sound inside the four walls

critter—informal word for creatures ranging from a wolf to a spider

dandy tricks of discipline—creative ways old timers took care of a problem

dead hoofer—a bad dancer

dinner—meal at mid-day

duds—casual term for clothing

dust had settled—when things calm down after a hullabaloo

dust him off—give an animal a scare to get rid of him

equine—relating to a horse

farm implements—equipment, pulled by horses to work the fields into production fiddlesticks—an old-fashioned expression of disagreement or mild anger

field dress—the process of removing the entrails from the body of a game animal

fish wheel—powered by the river current, a piece of equipment that scoops fish from water, dropping them into a bin for processing

flipped his wig—to lose one's composure or reason

fracas—noisy activity or a brawl

geezer—an old person

going outside—slang in Alaska for going on a journey out of the 49th state

got his nerve up—made up his mind to complete the task being faced

grit—firmness of mind or spirit, unyielding courage

greenhorn—inexperienced or naïve person

gumption—common sense, discerning, motivating awareness

handle—cowboy slang for a name

hanky-panky—improper behavior

harped on—emphasize, make a strong point

haywire—stops working, something goes wrong

hill potatoes—to hoe dirt around all sides of a potato plant to keep the tubers covered

horse tack—equipment and accessories used on horses or other equines

hullabaloo—loud noise and insistent utterings

humdinger—a striking or extraordinary thing or person

in a pickle or a bind—in a very difficult situation or an embarrassing position jarhead—nickname for a Marine

know the ropes—to know how a particular job is done

learning the ropes—the special way things are done in a particular place or activity

leatherneck—nickname for Marine

look-see—find out what is going on

loped along—taking long, methodical steps, not too fast or too slow

lower forty-eight—slang term Alaskans use for the other contiguous US states

moniker—a nickname

mouthful—using few words to make a big statement

Movietone News—newsreel that ran from 1928-1963 in the US

noggin—a humorous description of the head

on the peck—looking for a fight

on the trot—busy with activities

outside—term Alaskans use to describe going somewhere out of the 49th state

potluck—a group activity where people gather together and bring food to share for a meal

pumpjack—a ground-based drive for an inground pump, operated with a long handle to bring water to the surface

prove up—to show requirements for receiving a patent for government land have been completed

put your foot down—to adopt a firm policy when faced with opposition or disobedience

rough sledding—a difficult or troublesome period

rustle up—to find or get something together; prepare food quickly sack out—go to bed

saddle horse—a horse kept for riding only

saved our necks—to rescue one from disaster or prevent something bad from happening

set up housekeeping—acquiring supplies for a new place to live

Seward's Icebox—term critical of the purchase of Alaska by US Secretary of State, William Seward in 1867 for approximately 2¢ per acre

shanks' ponies—a person's legs, for walking

shindig—large or lavish party

sidekicks—friends

sniped—make a sly or petty verbal attack

soda jerk—typically a young man who operated a soda fountain in a drug store, preparing soda drinks or ice cream sodas

soddy—a basic house on the prairie built of grass sod blocks

Sourdough—a seasoned Alaska resident

spigot—a device used to control water flow from a crock, barrel or pipe

spooked—surprised

spring—an outlet for fresh, clear water flowing from the ground

Squaw candy—salmon that has been smoked or dried for a long time until it is very chewy, food for people and dogs

supper—the evening meal

TAPS—an acronym for Trans Alaska Pipeline System

threw in with us—to join one's activity

Title IX—provided equal access to girls in sports

tough sledding—a very difficult situation to work through

turned his crank—caused excitement

twang—quick motion to move a spring or musical string

varmints—a wild animal or bird considered a pest

worth his salt—worthy of your respect, especially because of a job well done

Chapter 1

THE BEGINNING

"Kenny, this isn't the game for you. It's for big men. Tall men!"

With that, six-foot-five Bud Sailors swatted yet another basketball shot from the hands of his younger brother Kenny. The worn basketball hit the packed dirt of the wind-blown Wyoming farm yard. Kenny scrambled through the dust and snagged the frayed ball as it bounced off the wooden backboard mounted on the wooden windmill in the corral.

Kenny said, "I was only five-foot-seven and five years younger than my brother. I was determined to make another attempt to get around Bud and drive into the iron hoop."

"I knew my chances were not high I'd ever get a shot off. The big bum Bud always stuffed the ball down my throat."

Kenny recalled, "The windmill was important to us as we scratched out a living on a dryland farm near Hillsdale, Wyoming in the 1930s. When the windmill was in gear and the wind blew, it pumped water through a metal pipe to the stock tank to water the animals. By moving a lever, fresh water was channeled from the pipe to a spigot for us to collect and use. The only way the water came into the house was one bucket at a time, carried at the end of somebody's arm. Water was critical for life. Period."

The Prairie Sentinel became a symbol of persistence for Kenny and would help establish his path to move forward in life.

Kenny commented: "I think the good Lord must have put it in my mind, to jump against Bud. I knew there had to be a way. I just had to figure it out."

Necessity became the mother of invention, and the result was to jump and shoot.

"I kept experimenting with quick moves until I found a way to shoot around that bum. When I changed my tactics, it made a difference in my shot. When I changed my shot, it made a difference in my game. I had no idea it would change the game of basketball forever."

Bud's little brother did become a difference-maker on the basketball court. Kenny continued to make a difference in the lives of other folks, long after he left the basketball courts.

Back to the backboard...that was another story. While not essential for life, it was mighty important in the development of two young fellows guided into manhood by a single mother with limited assets. Cora Houtz Sailors was one plucky lady. Raised in that sod house on the prairie, this woman was full of gumption. She persevered in the worst life threw at her. With her solid foundation of faith and determination, she was convinced she would ultimately prevail. The results? Both of her sons went on to raise families and succeed in the military and business.

Kenny said, "Bud and I competed hard against each other in the corral. Before we could play, we cleared out the cow chips and horse biscuits that decorated our fancy playing 'court.'"

"On a spring day as the wind howled across the grasslands," Kenny recalled, "I made up my mind I was going to find a way to shoot the ball over my brother and hit the hoop."

Bud, on the other hand, had another plan.

He stated, "I wanted to frustrate that little squirt and refuse him a chance for a single shot."

Kenny responded with, "I knew I could jump. I figured if I could jump high enough out of my dribble, I might get the ball up over the 'big Bud' problem."

He worked hard with that thought in mind.

"I'd dribble up, get around the dribble, jump straight up, bring the ball just above my head, and let it fly. It missed the backboard and hoop a few times. But then, by golly—that old basketball, finally dropped through the hoop on that rough wooden backboard."

Kenny was just as surprised as his brother was when the ball found its mark.

Bud recalled. "I was stunned to see the ball hit the hoop! My own feet were still planted in the dirt of the corral. I told my brother, you have to get better. You must get better at that."

Kenny said, "I started working hard to make that shot. I practiced dribbling and shooting with a leather basketball Bud had brought home from the high school in Hillsdale."

Bud had approached his Hillsdale basketball coach Floyd Domine.

"If we could have a ball to use," he explained, "we could practice when we have a little time in between chores."

"We?"

"That would be me and Kenny."

After some discussion, Domine gave his consent.

Having a basketball to use inspired the brothers to practice with dogged determination.

Bud Sailors was one of the best high school players in Wyoming and Domine valued this solid six-foot-five asset to the Hillsdale Basketball team. He also recognized Kenneth as the scrappy ball player from the early morning free-for-all ball sessions in the school gym. It looked like the hound dogs on the surrounding farms, frantically chasing the ever-present jackrabbits in the area.

"I was frequently at the head of the bunch of kids," Kenny commented. "The jackrabbit racing against the hounds, so to speak."

The students ran in frantic circles to keep ahead of the pursuers. It was a rare moment when one of the other players could steal the ball away from Bud's faster brother.

Later, when he played ball in high school, college, and the NBA, Kenny Sailors the runt, would take all sorts of hits from big men guarding the hoop. The gritty lessons of his youth in the dirt corral at home and the gym at school stayed with him.

Domine, along with the folks in the community, had watched for two years, as Bud rode his horse bareback the four miles into town each evening for basketball practice. Both boys possessed perseverance. Cora was adamant about her boys riding horses bareback. "I don't want either of you ridin' saddle. I've seen too many accidents because of saddles."

Kenny said, "Mother laid down that law when we first begged for horses to ride. There was no point in arguing with her. We continued to walk or ride bareback."

Chapter 2

HOUTZ HERITAGE

Kenny's Grandfather, David D. Houtz, was a noteworthy person in the family of Cora Belle Houtz Sailors. Born in the mid-1800s, he was trained as an educator in a New York state college. He headed to the Great Plains to seek his fortune in Nebraska. Houtz met and married Mary E. Vice.

According to Kenny. "My mother Cora was born June 8, 1881, in Nemaha County Nebraska. She had a sister and two brothers.

"Grandpa moved everyone on to Kansas where they had a farm and built a house called a 'soddy.' The walls were made of blocks of cut sod, stacked one on top of the other. The compact building had a packed dirt floor and one window. It was common to have varmints and snakes drop in from the walls or ceiling. Even rattlesnakes! Grandpa later heard about a teaching job out in Colorado and decided to leave the farm for the mining region."

In 1896 a fire devastated the mining camp of Cripple Creek, Colorado, where around 20,000 residents lived. With the rebuilding of the site, the townsfolk wanted schools and other amenities for their families.

"Grandpa Houtz was hired as one of the first teachers in the rough-and-tumble town. The family endured a difficult, month-long trip by covered wagon before they arrived at their destination.

"Grandpa got the teaching job because he was not only trained, he was also a big guy. A tough, towering disciplinarian, Grandpa stood six-foot-four and weighed 230-240 pounds. He was hired to straighten out a bunch of students that ranged in age from six to twenty-five. One of the problems in those days for teachers was the fact that these older boys could go to school as long as they could stand it. Some of them were big and up to no good. This group of mischief makers had already run off several teachers.

"Those miserable young men were bullies who had been trying to destroy the school system in the community. They had beaten up former teachers, thereby robbing the community of their investment in the education system. The smaller students suffered all types of physical abuse and humiliation at the hands of the older roughnecks as well. Cripple Creek residents were desperate for a way to bring order to the school, so all students could thrive, and families would know their children as well as the teachers would be safe."

On the first day of school, Mr. Houtz lined everyone up outside the building and made a statement: "I understand several of you older boys have had a lot of fun runnin' off teachers."

The big guys smirked.

"We might as well get this thing straightened out right now." Houtz paused. "Do any of you think you can run me off?"

The oldest student stepped forward—a bearded, surly lout, who smiled confidently.

"Yeah, I think we can," he sneered at the older man.

Not batting an eye, the teacher took a quick step forward, delivered a swift punch to the solar plexus of the student, and down he went. Flat on his back.

Rubbing one hand over the other, Houtz surveyed the stunned group: "Is there anybody else?" The other students sucked in their breath and stepped back. Mr. Houtz had no more problems during his tenure at Cripple Creek. The learning process went on to flourish.

Kenny said, "Grandpa was a teacher who meant business and yet cared about his students. He went on to develop ways to gain control over difficult situations in primitive classroom settings. As a result, his students received a good education and the parents were grateful."

"We heard stories of discipline during the years of frontier schools. Common punishments for schoolroom infractions included twisting an ear, lifting (or pulling the hair) at the nape of the neck, or applying a ruler to an outstretched hand. Grandpa Houtz was a well-respected teacher who used common sense in how he maintained classroom order."

The whole exercise in behavioral management was not lost on his young daughter Cora. Later in life, she must have reached back into the bag of tricks that her father had developed and pulled out some dandies as she guided her sons.

"She made it clear to us," Kenny related, "that expectations would be met at home or in school. You needed to pay attention, be respectful, and do your best. Period."

Kenny continued. "My mother probably finished out her education at that time in Colorado. When she completed the *McGuffey Reader* #6 and participated in the common exams, she did well. The exams were very comprehensive and held the students to high standards. The whole business of finishing the *McGuffey Reader* series was a very big deal and something both Mother and her father were proud of."

"After a few years, Grandpa decided to return to Nebraska and teach there."

The family left Cripple Creek and ended up in the very southeast corner of Nebraska, in Falls City. He stayed in the classroom until 1905, when he became superintendent of schools in Nebraska. He held that position until he retired in 1920. His sons Elmer and Melvin lived close by, near Verdon. Grandpa purchased a small country store and settled down.

"It was in Falls City that my mother met my father, Edward Talbert Sailors," Kenny said. "Dad had been born in Wabash, Indiana, on March 30, 1878, and made his way west to Nebraska. My parents were married on March 6, 1900."

Chapter 3

CORA'S FAMILY

After Kenny's parents married, they moved to a farm near Verdon, Nebraska, very close to where Cora had been born. Their first daughter, Gladys, was born in December of 1900. She told the story of their early family life in the *Hillsdale Heritage Book* of 1976.

Gladys wrote; "I had just turned ten years old when Mother gave birth to triplet daughters in December of 1910. They weighed a total of less than eleven pounds. The smallest baby didn't even weigh three pounds and lived only a few hours. I stayed out of school the rest of that term to help at home. We bottle-fed the babies using little rocks to shake around inside the narrow-neck bottles to get them clean. We were so exhausted that no one felt like cooking. The only food we ate was what the neighbors brought to us.

"The two babies who survived developed what was called 'three months colic.' Mamma and Dad took care of them during the day. At night I'd carry one little girl on my shoulder and jiggle the other in the baby buggy. Those babies screamed and screamed. One of them lived for fourteen months and the other eighteen months. It was a horrible time."

The names of the babies were not even noted.

"After the babies died, Dad decided to purchase a butcher shop and a nice home in Verdon. Mamma was very efficient and helped him operate the business. She was active in the community and involved in the church. My brother Barton, or 'Bud,' was born in 1916. The next year, Dad bought a section of land in the western part of Nebraska, south of Bushnell.

"In 1919, I married Archie Smith and lived near my folks. Our daughter, Vera, was born in 1920, and another daughter, Irma, in 1921."

Kenny was born at home on the family farm on January 14, 1921.

"Dad was not happy with Mother," Gladys stated. "He decided that there were just too many mouths to feed and figured he'd throw the new baby to the pigs and get rid of him. He took tiny Kenny and headed out the door."

Gladys couldn't stand what was about to happen. She had to do something!

Running after her father she grabbed his arm.

"Dad, you just can't do that! Think about it. This is your son!"

Gladys was determined to stand for what was right and ultimately prevailed in the family crisis. The life of her baby brother was spared.

Soon after, Ed Sailors left the family and never returned.

Kenny said, "My mother eventually found out he was chasing around with other women and divorced him."

The family later found out Edward had died of cancer in 1959 while living in Missouri.

With Ed gone, Cora was left in a difficult situation. She decided the best thing to do would be to sell the farm and move in with her father back in Falls City. She packed up the boys and headed east across the state, to Falls City, Nebraska.

Grandpa Houtz needed help with his store and Cora's family needed a home. The arrangement worked out for everyone. Cora and the boys had a secure place to live and Grandpa would have company plus help with the store.

Bud (L) and Kenny (R) in front of the store of Grandpa Houtz. 1926. (Photo courtesy of Sailors family.)

Kenny had stories to tell about D.D. Houtz. "Grandpa often sat in the rocker near the potbellied stove in the store and got a kick out of playing checkers or talking with customers. He had many opinions about the state of the country, and would commence to give anyone around that bulging, cast iron heater an earful."

"In 1926, Grandpa Houtz died of a heart attack in his rocker," Kenny remembered. "Mother continued to run the store and kept a stiff upper lip. Grit moved her forward to keep on, and determination guided her to do the best she could to make a living and raise us boys."

Cora decided she wanted to get her sons out on a farm where they could learn the value of hard work and stay out of trouble. She knew it would be a life of deprivation and hardship, but she was willing to pay the price to raise decent young men.

The family planned an auction sale of household goods for November 12, 1930. County records showed that Cora sold the store property on December 20, 1930. With the money from the store, Cora decided it would be to their advantage to be near her daughter. Gladys and her family had moved to a farm in southwest Wyoming, near Egbert.

The family story continued in the *Hillsdale Heritage* book, as told by Gladys.

"After Mama sold Grandpa's store, she and the boys stayed with us for several months."

Kenny remembered the time spent together. "I enjoyed the company of my sister and her family. Bud and I were kept busy with chores on the large potato farm that Archie and Gladys had."

"Archie was one of the first farmers to use the new iron-wheeled tractors, a very impressive piece of equipment at that time. He had a crew that would travel around the area, hiring out to other farmers, who were willing to pay for his services in their fields."

Perhaps this experience planted seeds in the mind of young Kenneth who had a way of "putting his thinking cap on." He had the chance to figure out how to get around old problems and come up with new solutions.

Cora scouted the area for a place of her own, where she could make a living and raise the boys on a farm. She believed this type of life would develop her sons into more resilient and wholesome men.

Kenny recalled, "Mother located a farm four miles south of Hillsdale, Wyoming, which suited her. She was able to buy the place in 1931 with the inheritance from her father's store. There was a two-story house with no central heating, an outhouse, a chicken coop, a barn, a corral with a windmill, and a stock tank for water. An ample garden space was available with a shed for storing dried cow chips and pieces of rubber tires, which we would use to stoke the stoves during cold weather."

The purchase price of the 300 acres included all of the equipment, a team of workhorses, a few head of cattle, several pigs, a flock of chickens, and even the dog. Seventy-five acres of that land would be used to grow crops, while the rest was pasture land for the cows and horses. An old wooden windmill loomed up on the west side of the corral. That prairie sentinel became much more than wind energy to the developing young men.

"Times were tough for Mama and the boys, as it was for most folks. But she wasn't about to give up. She trusted God to take care of them," Gladys recalled. "A new road was to be built near their new home. A gravel sale to the State Highway Department was negotiated and brought in a bit of much-needed cash for her at a critical time."

Chapter 4

MAKING MEN IN THE GREAT DEPRESSION

During the spring planting season, the boys had vivid memories of leaving for school in the morning. With emotion, Kenny described Cora as he and Bud boarded the school bus during that time.

"Mother would be driving the team of workhorses into the field when we climbed on the bus in the morning. We would watch her grow smaller in the distance as the vehicle rolled down the road and away from the farm. She was bundled up with a heavy coat, scarf, gloves, and heavy shoes. It was hard to stay warm in the ferocious winds that blew across the plains. Mother was determined to do her job so we could make a living. She was quite a woman."

The winds that screamed across the high plains of Wyoming were piercing and brutal. Often, they would be accompanied by freezing sleet or stinging snow storms. It was imperative to get crops planted into the fields as the soil warmed—and before the hoped-for rains might come. Cora knew she had to do what she had to do, no matter what. She never complained about her task. She just did it. The boys knew what their mother did for them and learned that actions do have consequences. She was a role model for determinations and long-suffering. The lessons Bud and Kenny learned from Cora, were caught, not taught.

In the late afternoon, as they stepped off the bus at the end of the school day, Bud and Kenny would see their mother, still at work in the field. She would be hunched over the reins attached to the harnesses of the plodding team of workhorses, still moving forward.

When wishful thinking came about the tractor Archie had on his farm, the family made the best of what they had to work with, a faithful team of draft horses.

Through all the sacrifices, the boys knew their mother loved them. They saw and felt the depth of her commitment.

There were many chores on the farm. Everyone pitched in to get them done daily. Taking care of the chickens. Milking the cows. Feeding the pigs and other animals. Hauling water from the windmill to the house. Making sure to pump water into the stock tank, if the wind had gone quiet. Keeping the coal and sawdust supplies prepared for the stoves. Kerosene and coal oil lamps needed to be prepared to provide light in the dark days of fall and winter. Pieces of old rubber tires were picked from the roadsides to burn for fuel. Dried cow chips were collected from the pastures and corrals to be added to the storehouse. These extra materials would be burned in times when coal ran low.

Kenny talked of the cold. "Those pieces of rubber would burn hot in the stove. It seemed like we were always cold in the winter."

"When Mother was young, she picked up cow chips to burn. We did the same thing. Having anything to burn was important."

"Bud and I slept upstairs in the same bed. In cold weather, Mother would pile whatever extra bedding she had on us. There were plenty of cracks in the walls of our house and no insulation. The freezing winds of the Wyoming countryside always found their way inside the walls. It was cold. Mother slept downstairs in a room off of the kitchen, so she could keep the fire stoked during the night."

A personal habit Cora passed on to her sons was regular Bible reading.

Kenny said, "The fact that Mother read to us from Scriptures every night, was something that stuck with me throughout my life. There were times, I slacked off in that regard, but I would return to the Word and begin to read it again. It was something I needed."

"Mother would close her prayers with, 'Thy will be done and not mine.' I began to add that truth to my prayers as I grew older. Even though it was difficult at times, I learned His ways were far better than mine."

.....

There was fieldwork in the spring and summer. Raising potatoes, corn, and beans, plus taking care of a big garden. In those times, if you were to eat, you had to work. No way around it. There were parallels between cultivating land and life. Both needed special attention to produce results. The produce, or grains, resulted in food for people and animals. Hard-working and honest people resulted in productive lives and good citizens.

Times did come when there would be a break in the ever-present work. When that happened, the boys would high-tail it for the dirt corral. The ball would be lobbed at the wooden backboard with the iron hoop Bud had nailed to the windmill. The corral was a place of freedom and reckless abandon where those brothers went at it. Kenny was always on the scramble. His shots were blocked, and drives to the hoop were thwarted. He continued to work on improving his dribbling skills and quickness, always watching the Bud for direction and encouragement.

Kenny couldn't match Bud's height advantage, but that didn't stop him from trying. He continued to work on building his dribbling skills and quickness. Bud refused to make it easy on the squirt and would not let up on his little brother. Kenny just kept trying. And trying. And trying.

Chapter 5

GETTING BY

An old school bus rattled and chugged its way around the dirt road near the Sailors' place, collecting kids from outlying farms and ranches.

Kenny said, "The students would be hauled into town and dropped off at the Hillsdale public school. The route had a varied schedule. The bus would come from one direction for a few days, and then the route would be reversed. That way the same students were not always last on—last off.

"We learned, with that bus schedule, there were some days we would arrive at school earlier. When we arrived early, the principal allowed us to play basketball in the gym.

"It was in those free-for-all scrimmages, that I learned to dribble. The rules of the gym were simple: whoever got their mitts on the ball and kept dribbling, was in the driver's seat. It was little kids and big kids, no holds barred. Everyone was desperately running around the hardwood, seeking to keep that old laced-up ball, in their control."

"I built skills that later helped me guide and direct high school, college, and professional basketball teams."

We made our own rules, but we played by them. I look back on those opportunities and realize how much I learned early on. Being able to dribble, make contact, and still control the ball became a strength for me. Those kids would practically take you down, jump on you, and do whatever they could to try to get the ball away. You had to keep dribbling if you wanted the ball.

" I wanted that ball."

"My mother grew up in very difficult circumstances. With all the challenges of just trying to stay alive, she learned early on, that emotions would have to be pushed aside. The idea of being controlled and self-sufficient was the message we got from her.

"At the time, Bud and I may not have realized the importance of those foundational traits. I think they became building blocks for future success. Being in control of emotions, was key in how he and I learned to make good decisions. It didn't matter where we ended up. In critical moments, we would control our emotions, contain excitement or fear, and do what we had been trained to do. Whether hoeing a row of potatoes, shooting a basketball, or quick judgment calls in combat, we kept our eyes on the goal.

"Yes, there was a lot of character-building taking place as we grew up on the farm. Chores built character. Believe me, we had plenty of chores that had to be done. Everyone pitched in to get the jobs done daily, whether we liked it or not. We had to take care of chickens two times a day and also pick the eggs. The cows needed to be milked twice a day. All of the other animals needed to be fed morning and night. Water needed to be hauled from the windmill into the house. We had to make sure to pump water into the stock tank for all of the animals to drink. If the wind had gone quiet, we needed to hand pump water into the stock tank. It was important to keep the coal and sawdust supplies ready for use in the stove.

"Bud and I probably didn't realize it at the time, but Mother knew what it would take, to shape us into men who could be trusted to get the job done.

"Field work had to be done in season. Before the early rains came in the spring, the land would have to be plowed, disked, and harrowed before it could be planted with seed. In the summer, some of the fields needed to be cultivated with a plow or a hand hoe. At the end of summer or in early autumn, it was time to harvest the crops. After all of the work, you'd hope to have a crop such as beans or potatoes that you could sell for cash. Hay was either piled into stacks or stored in the barn. The wheat, oats, or barley went into bins for animal feed. Potatoes. carrots, turnips. and beets were stored in the house cellar. With all of the crops, it was always a race against the weather, to beat freezing temperatures and early snow storms.

"It was important to have a garden. A family needed to plant and harvest a variety of vegetables, which would produce enough food to see them through the year. The bottom line was, that you must produce your food to survive. If you were going to eat you had to work. No way around it. Yet, times would come when there with a break in the work activities. When that happened, Bud and I would high-tail it for the corral with the iron hoop on the side of the windmill. Believe me, we made the most of any opportunities that came our way."

Chapter 6

LESSONS LEARNED

Money was always in short supply with the Sailors family. Cora thought about ways they could bring in extra dollars. Since her daughter Gladys and her family raised potatoes, Cora decided she and the boys should give that a try. The following spring, they planted 40 acres of spuds. Those tubers had to be weeded and hilled using handheld hoes. This was a slow and backbreaking process that took scores of hours. The trio would be out in the rows of plants, working together for many long days, before the job was completed.

Kenny said, "Mother always showed us how to hold the hoe and remove the weeds. She would watch us and then expect we'd do the job—right."

One day when Kenneth was nine years old he had it with that tiresome job. He turned to his mother, lifted his hoe to his shoulder, and stated: "I'm going to quit. I'm tired and I don't want to hoe anymore."

Cora straightened up, leaned on her hoe, gave Kenny a long look, and said: "Okay Kenneth, take your hoe and leave. Just don't come to the supper table tonight. Remember the Bible says, 'If anyone will not work, neither shall he eat.' [II Thes. 3:10 NKJ] Just take your hoe and leave."

He could not believe his ears. No supper! "I knew my mother meant what she said, and I was hungry. There was nothing more to say."

The young man turned back to hoeing in the next row over from his mother. He didn't like it at the time but recognized that his mother loved him enough to set boundaries and teach him that rewards come with effort. Both Kenny and Bud knew that anything their mother asked them to do, she did first and stayed with the job until it was finished. Period.

.....

The boys figured their Grandpa Houtz had taught their mother how to raise kids with solid correction. The result was a woman without a husband who was able to raise boys. Cora did not hesitate to administer swift discipline when necessary.

Kenny remembered some of the punishment. "One day Mother heard Bud cussing out in the farmyard. She grabbed him by the hair at the nape of his neck and marched him into the kitchen. Then proceeded to wash his mouth out with homemade lye soap.

Through the frothing soap bubbles, Bud managed to sputter out, "Mother, I'll never cuss again. I'll never cuss again!"

Kenny made up his mind he would not cuss either. The lesson hit home with both of the boys. Decades later, Kenny said, "To this day I haven't heard my brother cuss. I don't cuss either."

"On Sunday mornings we'd go to a small white clapboard, steepled Methodist church in town," Kenny recalled. "My job was to bring the team into the barn. Bud and I would hitch the horses to the wagon and we'd all climb aboard. Mother and Bud sat on the wooden seat. I parked on a log stump in the back. We bounced and jolted over the four miles of dirt road. The only time we missed was if the weather was bad. Gathering together for worship was important, not only for our spiritual lives but to participate in community life.

"Another important activity for me in the summertime was to take my dog and gun to hunt rabbits for fresh meat. The young rabbits were tender. We thought they tasted better than chicken. When I brought in older jackrabbits, Mother boiled them and made canned mincemeat to use during the year. We knew we had to preserve food when we had the chance."

Now that hound dog, Shep, was a fine companion for a young boy, and Kenny loved him. However, there could be problems with that pooch. When Cora caught the dog in the chicken house sucking eggs, she said: "Kenneth, we've got to teach that old dog a lesson. We can't have him eating eggs that we need to trade for food at the store."

"Oh no! You're not going to shoot him, are you Mother?"

"Of course not. Here's what we'll do. Let's soft boil an egg that you'll put in one of the nests. We'll let the dog sneak into the chicken coop."

The egg was cooked up and Kenny placed the hot cackleberry in the nest. He and his mother kept watch from the house. As expected, the old dog snuck into the coop. Before long they heard a "yipe – yipe," from the inside of the little building. Chickens flew around as the dog burst through the door, hot eggshell stuck to his lips!

"How about that?" Cora looked at Kenny with a twinkle in her eyes. "I don't think we'll have to worry about that dog eating any more of our eggs."

Kenny was amazed at how smart his mother was. "She handled an ordinary situation in an unusual, but very effective way."

Such a clever response. It was one more seed of ingenuity planted in the mind of a young boy, developing into a future difference-maker.

Chapter 7

STATE OF FLUX

Never underestimate the power of lessons learned while picking corn.

Kenny recalled, "When we harvested corn, Bud drove the team of horses, which pulled a wagon down the side of the field. Mother and I would pick the ears of corn in adjacent rows and toss them over into the wagon. After all the corn was brought out of the field, Bud and I loaded up and went to town to peddle the ears. We sold them for 10¢ a dozen."

While working in the corn field one day, Shep let out a howl that let everyone know he was onto a rabbit. Cora exclaimed to Kenny. "Now get yourself over into the other row and catch that rabbit. I'll fix him for supper." Kenny hightailed it to where he heard the racket.

After the fracas, Kenny gave an account. "When I broke out of the corn stalks, the rabbit was plowing straight toward me. He didn't see me because his eyes were rolled back as he was trying to watch the dog. I grabbed him by the ears as he tore by. That ol' rabbit was fighting and scratching me and then, the dog was on me. Trying to get to the rabbit! Above it all, I heard Mother hollering, 'Hold on Kenny. I'm coming.'"

Well, he did and she did and they had rabbit for supper.

While they ate that night, the family discussed how they might acquire a saddle horse.

"We don't have the money to buy a horse," said Bud. "I'll see if I can work for one."

Sure enough, a deal was made. Bud held up his end of the bargain and found a job with a neighbor. The man held up his end of the bargain and gave Bud a horse as payment for a job well done. That mare made the trips back and forth to basketball practice a lot quicker and easier for the young man.

"Even better," Kenny added, "the mare delivered a foal soon after arriving at our place. Mother told me the new horse would be mine, but I'd have to learn to train and break the pony."

Ever the entrepreneur, Cora figured out another way to make extra money.

"Okay boys, we can bring in some cash money by selling pork."

The family went to work once more, this time increasing the number of hogs they would raise for sale.

"It was a big undertaking," Kenny related. "When the hogs reached around 200 pounds, we butchered them and cut them up in quarters. Mother rustled up clean, white sheets. The fresh meat was wrapped and loaded into an old Model A Ford car we'd managed to get our hands on. Mother sent Bud and me into Cheyenne. We worked our way up and down the streets of the city, knocking on doors, and offering our pork to prospective customers. We didn't quit until all the meat was sold and the Model A was empty."

The effort and hard work paid off, Kenny added. "We had more money that summer than we'd ever had before in our lives."

"Mother then decided, we needed fresh pork for our family," Kenny recalled. "One morning she said to Bud, 'Take the gun, go out and shoot a pig so we can have meat for supper.' Bud commenced shooting. Shooting and missing. Mother marched over, grabbed the gun, took aim, and killed the pig with one shot. She didn't mess around."

Maybe it was the extra money from the pork project that created a miserable opportunity for Kenny. Cora liked the violin and thought Kenneth should learn to play the instrument. To say it was a struggle for all involved would have been an understatement. Kenny's agony went on for a short time before the violin teacher made a special trip to the farm.

The man informed Cora, "Stop wasting your money. Kenneth is no musician."

When Cora started to object, Bud stepped in. "Mother, you might as well sell that violin and buy the kid a single-shot .22 rifle. He could take the old hound dog hunting and bring home some meat."

Cora was between a rock and a hard spot. The violin was sold and a rifle was purchased. That was one of the few times she ever relented and changed her mind.

"A rifle, a dog, and a horse. I was on top of the world," the former music student stated. "I did a lot better with the rifle than with that old violin anyway."

In 1934, Cora decided the boys needed more than a high school education. She said, "Bud, next year you're going to go to college in Laramie at the University of Wyoming." Turning to her youngest son she added, "When you're old enough, Kenneth, you'll go to college too. We will be selling the farm in order to move to town."

Kenny's response was guarded. "I didn't know what to think. We boys hadn't been off the farm much except for peddling corn and pork. Other than going to church on Sundays and school during the week, our experience was limited."

In the spring of 1935, Bud finished high school and Kenny completed eighth grade. The Hillsdale Associated School District celebrated graduation and the end of school.

Kenny spoke with delight: "This was the most highly anticipated event of the year for the community. It was a lot of fun for everyone! There was a big picnic for the whole community which the Superintendent organized. Everyone pitched in and brought something to eat. And boy, there was plenty of food and nobody went home hungry.

"After we ate, recalled Kenny, there were games and races to participate in. I challenged myself to keep up and even beat some of the older kids in the races. That day was the high point of our year."

.....

A buyer for the farm was located and the place was sold. There was one final, sticky detail for Kenny. Cora informed her son, "Some men came to the house today. They are going to buy your horse for $45."

"I could not believe what I was hearing," lamented Kenny. "I had raised Paint from birth. I trained that pony to respond to my commands and come at my whistle. She was mighty special to me."

Kenny's voice broke as he continued, "Riding my horse bareback to the train station and loading her into a boxcar was the hardest thing I'd had to do in my life. I gave her a last hug and stepped away. She was headed to Green River. I didn't look back.

"Later, I did tell Bud that I may have shed a tear or two."

Chapter 8

LARAMIE

Cora flat-out told the boys, "Life has to move on. No sense in wasting time worrying over it. There will be new opportunities for you in town."

As usual, Cora Sailors guided her sons through what needed to be done to make the next change and further their education.

The money from the sale of the farm, Kenny's horse, and a bumper crop of potatoes from the fields made it possible to purchase a large three-story house in Laramie. The home had a reasonable kitchen and several bedrooms which would be rented to university students. Cora would cook meals for their boarders.

Kenny recalled, "Bud and I could not figure out what in the world was going on. Life was so much different in town. But Mother had a plan that worked and we made a good living."

Cora realized her children did not have the life experiences to make far-reaching decisions. She was not afraid to stand in the gap and be an example to help them make solid decisions.

Living in town was an adjustment. With no extra money, Kenny had to make do with the clothes he had.

"When I showed up at school wearing bib overalls, the students of Laramie High made it a point to make my life miserable. I figured I wouldn't stand for somebody picking on me over something as dumb as a pair of bib overalls. I was willing to do what it took to convince them. Even if it meant a fight. I had a sense of what was right or wrong.

"I was like most other kids and just wanted people to like me and pay attention to me. Not make fun of me.

"I gathered my nerve up. Mother, I'd like to have some waist overalls to wear to school, so the other kids will quit teasing me."

Cora's response was a flat no.

Bud stepped in on behalf of his brother.

"Mother, I have a little extra cash I could spend on some Levi waist pants for him."

This was one of the few times Cora relented. Bud bought the pants. Kenny wore them.

Once Kenny was on the basketball court, it didn't take the critics long to pay attention to the new athlete. The other fellows on the team began to notice what this country bumpkin could do on the hardwood floors. This time, the attention was positive and didn't cease.

Chapter 9

TOWN LIFE

With renters in the house, the family had actual cash, in hand.

Kenny commented, "It was very unusual for us to have money in the house when we lived on the farm. We existed by bartering. Cash of any amount was something special."

The family joined the First Christian Church in Laramie, where they were embraced by a wonderful group of friends. Faith was so important to Cora, and the new fellowship was indeed a blessing for her.

The boys recognized how much their mother had given up for them and were happy she had a chance to do something for herself.

Kenny remembered with fondness, "She was often on the trot with her new friends. Bud and I were glad to see her take advantage of new opportunities and even have the chance to have a little fun. Her life had not been easy."

On one side of the new house was a concrete driveway. Bud said to the squirt, "Let's put up a basketball hoop out there. We can get extra shooting practice in that way."

Basketball wasn't the only shooting that went on for the family. Kenny would head out to the foothills around town and hunt cotton-tail rabbits. "I also hunted pheasants in the weeds and grass along the fence lines in season. I didn't exactly bring home the bacon, but we'd eat every last bite of game I brought in. Nothing went to waste in our family."

Kenny liked to say, "My mom could shoot. A gun, that is. Not a basketball."

Kenny was fourteen when he saw his first big game animal.

"It was a hot day in the fall of the year," He explained. "My new friends had asked me to go along on an antelope hunt. We drove about forty miles out of Laramie, along the foothills of the Laramie Range of the Rocky Mountains. It was a different kind of hunt than any I'd been on before. An antelope, or pronghorn, was a much bigger animal than a jackrabbit."

The situation was a surprise to Kenny. "You could see the animals in the distance and they didn't run until we started sneaking up on them. Antelope are curious. If you get down and stay quiet for a while, they eventually come to look you over." He tucked that information away for use years later during sheep hunts in Alaska. "Use something to create a little flag. Make the animal curious and they'll wander over."

"We were able to entice an antelope close enough for a shot. Wouldn't you know it, one of the other guys bagged the animal, but we all pitched in to field dress the antelope. We didn't do a great job—actually, it was a lousy job."

"Somehow, we managed to rupture the entrails in a few places. It's a messy job and it's not for the squeamish. There's no way around it. Comes with the territory."

The hunters finally finished the job and headed back to town. There, they were able to get more experienced help with cutting up the carcass. The meat was divided and shared to be enjoyed by all the families. Quite a memorable hunt for Kenny. He would not have another big game hunt until after he joined the Marines, completed college, and played professional basketball.

The principle of making sure to use any meat that was harvested, followed throughout Kenny's life and hunting career. He said, "I always told my hunters the same thing: If you kill an animal, you use it or give it away. *Don't* let anything go to waste."

Being a responsible person of integrity was deeply ingrained in Kenneth.

Indoor plumbing, electricity, and the conveniences of city life were not taken for granted by this family. City living on the High Plains was a far cry from the howling wind, isolation, and drudgery of life on the farm outside of Hillsdale. The Sailors family appreciated all aspects of these urban luxuries. "Especially the indoor bathroom and electric lights," Kenny would laugh.

Kenny drily remarked. "Being in a city of around 18,000 people was huge compared to Hillsdale with maybe 250 residents. Getting used to a city high school and a state university gave both Bud and me plenty of reasons to scratch our heads. Stepping away from a smaller school and into the fray of several hundred students was quite a deal."

Cora frequently reminded her boys, "It doesn't make any difference if you get knocked down seven times. *You get back up again.*" Getting back up was the way to move forward. Cora was not only interested in moving her life forward but in teaching her sons how to move their lives forward.

Those new Levi's Bud bought gave the unknown freshman an encouraging boost as he spread his wings and began making inroads into the high school student body.

Kenny would say, "I was a reasonable student I guess. At least I didn't flunk out." Sports were his main interest and his door to popularity in high school and college.

Chapter 10

CITY ADJUSTMENTS

Living in town was a real adjustment for Kenny. His mother was busy with the boarding house, and Bud was over his head trying to take university classes and attend basketball practice. He also drove a taxi at night to help with family finances. According to Kenny, "Mother had conditioned Bud and me for change. He and I made the best of it. We knew we could do no less."

Cora was happy to have found a church home to join in Laramie. The First Christian Church was close enough the family could walk to services each Sunday and attend other activities throughout the week. The boys were happy they didn't have to deal with the team of horses and wagon to get to town. Their mother was happy to have found a group of other spiritually minded folks.

The boys did chores to help Cora at the boarding house. Bud and Kenny helped with dishwashing, vacuuming, and cleaning. Nine young men roomed with them during the first year. Everyone ate together at a big table.

"I was glad we didn't have to use the scrub board to do the wash, as Mother did out on the farm," Kenny declared. "There was some kind of an 'automatic deal' we used to wash clothes. I never really knew what it was or how it worked. But it did get the clothes clean."

Kenny missed the outdoors and enjoyed times when he could take a hike away from town. In the 1930s it didn't take long to walk out of town. If he wasn't hunting, he made time to walk, sit down, and take in nature around him. He watched ants work in their hills. Observed the birds and animals around him in different months. He even stared into the skies and watched the clouds stream across the heavens, above the high plateau where Laramie spread out. In those quiet moments, Kenny saw ordinary activities that made sense to him.

He remarked, "Surrounded by the majesty of nature, it was hard for me to understand how a person could deny the existence of God. His handiwork is beyond anything man has ever tried to create. I found comfort and hope as I started a routine in a new school."

Laramie High School was the biggest building Kenny had ever been in. Two men in the building made a good impression on him. "I liked the principal, Mr. Thayer, right off. He made a point to reach out to me as the new kid from the farm. The high school coach, Floyd Foreman, was a real good man too. He was a gentleman, decent, had character, and knew how to deal with a bunch of goofy kids."

When Kenny didn't go out for football, Coach Foreman challenged him, "What's the matter Kenny, are you afraid to come out for football?"

"That's not it," Kenny responded. "Of course I'm not afraid. I just don't know anything about the game." The coach went right to work to teach him about the sport. With help from the quarterback, Kenny was placed in a good position as a left end, where he could use his speed and quickness. As was the custom, each team member played both ways—offense and defense.

He laughed as he recalled his time on the field. "I set up across the line from guys that weighed a lot more than I did. Coach Foreman taught me how to do a cross-body block. I'd throw my weight against the opponent instead of trying to wrestle him down."

Kenny described playing night games. "The folks that had cars would park them around the field with the headlights turned on so we could see. Once in a while, a light beam hit you right in the eye and blinded you for the play."

A school bus was used to haul the boys around to play neighboring schools such as Rawlins, Cheyenne, Pine Bluff, Wheatland, and Chugwater. Out of the area, their toughest competitors were Sheridan and Casper.

Floyd Foreman was a caring mentor to the young men around him. "At that time, a coach covered all of the sports: football, basketball, and track. I competed in each of them and lettered in all three sports."

Kenny was mighty grateful to this man. "He showed me what it was to be an excellent example of character, morality, and decency. Foreman showed us how to cooperate and not always force our way into a situation. He modeled how a good attitude would improve discipline and teamwork. Coach Foreman was a good man and had a big impact on my life."

Kenny described a fun pastime for the high school kids. "When there was any spare time and the weather was decent, we would high tail it out to Prexy's Pasture at the university. This grass field was north of Main Street and the scene of impromptu tackle football games. The group was mostly guys, but a few girls joined the crowd on occasion."

Kenny commented on the rowdy activity: "Sometimes, kids got whacked and even knocked out. I guess it wasn't too bad though, as no ambulance or public officials were called. It was just a lot of fun for us all.

"Football became my favorite sport in high school. I was a real brute at 138 pounds. I loved being able to move fast and get in and sack a quarterback. In my senior year, I was the top left end in the state."

When football season wound up, all focus turned to basketball. Coach Foreman allowed Kenny to use his unusual jump shot because he could score with it.

"I worked on developing that shot as I played. I thought about it a lot. I never saw another player try anything like what I did."

And what he did—no one could do better.

Chapter 11

HIGH SCHOOL JOBS

Before the end of the school year, Kenny was on the lookout for summer jobs. He chuckled as he talked about the work he ended up with while attending high school.

"My mother decided she'd had enough of the boarding house after a year. Her Aunt Hattie owned the Brooklyn Lodge twenty-four miles away in Centennial and hired Mother to cook and take care of guests at the lodge. Our big house was sold and we moved to a smaller home. Mother moved out to the lodge for the summer and Bud and I stayed in the new place."

"Bud had landed a job at the University of Wyoming Experiment Farm, where he worked on a crew that researched and developed different varieties of grains for the region. By that time, we had a car and he drove back and forth each day."

After work at the Farm one day, Bud had a question for Kenny: "Would you want to go to work at the Experiment Farm with me this summer?"

Kenny quickly replied, "Why, I'd go to work anywhere."

"Doctor Bass, the Farm director, wondered if they offered you a job, could you do a man's work? I told him, my brother is so cocky, he'll prove himself by outworking all of us."

Doctor Bass replied, 'Tell him to come. We'll hire him.'"

Kenny was thrilled.

"Bud and I moved out to live at the Experiment Farm. We were given a nice room in a storage building for a place to bunk, and we were set for the rest of that summer."

In the following two years, Cora had quit working at the Brooklyn Lodge and took a job cooking for haying crews on the ranch of Bucky Yarborough who lived in the area. This rancher had hundreds of horses and supplied most of the stock for the famous *Cheyenne Frontier Days* rodeo.

With the rodeo event in mind, Kenny's mother decided to talk to her boss.

"Mr. Yarborough, my son is good with horses and I'm wondering if you might be interested in hiring him for a haying crew?"

Yarborough liked Cora. "Bring your son along and I'll give him a chance to see if he's worth hiring."

On his first day on the job, Mr. Yarborough took Kenny out to a corral full of horses.

He shook out a lariat and said to the boy, "Let's catch you up some horses."

Kenny could only shake his head. "I had never roped a horse in my life up to that point!"

He followed the lead of the ranch owner. They brought in a team of work horses and hitched the pair to a waiting hay rake.

"Now Kenny, you have to understand these horses are sort of broke, but not real well trained. The teams are not used to being in the harness all day and can get a little ornery working in the fields. You'll be making windrows with the rake. I suppose we could say, it looks like a row of hay, heaped up by the wind."

Kenny watched and paid close attention to the boss as he handled the team.

"I knew how to drive a team of horses, but having that rake contraption hooked up was a completely different type of a deal."

With Kenny finally seated on the rake, Bucky gave him some advice: "Now, if the horses run away on you, just fall off the back of this rig. Let them go. If the team get tangled up and breaks the tongue on the rake, don't worry. We'll just fix it." This new kid on the haying crew raised his eyebrows and looked thoughtfully at Bucky Yarborough. With a sharp "giddyap," he snapped the reins and headed the team out to the field to do his best.

At the end of the day, the young Sailors drove his team back to the corral with the equipment and horses all in good shape. Bucky Yarborough gave him a "tip of the hat." Kenny was hired.

The teenager described work days on the ranch.

"We were up at dawn, ate breakfast, and headed out to the fields. A short break for dinner at noon and we were back to making hay."

"The hands came in around 5:30 pm. Everyone had chores to do before we could eat supper. Guys headed out to take care of calves, feed stock, or clean stalls and pens. After supper, we could relax before hitting the sack in the bunkhouse."

Speaking of the bunkhouse, Kenny added, "Being a fourteen-year-old kid living with a bunch of seasoned cowboys was quite an experience. Most of the crew were old hands and knew what they were doing. During the Great Depression, many fellas rode the rails from one place to another looking for work. Some were good honest men, down on their luck. Others were just bums.

"I'd never seen a poker game before. After supper one night, I stood behind a guy to watch. All of a sudden, this fella jumped up and accused me of signaling another cowboy across the table about his cards. I was flabbergasted.

"I guess that ol' guy thought he'd give me a good scare. And he did!"

"Mr. Bigmouth grabbed a gun off the wall and started to chase me. All I could think to do was run up to the ranch house. I busted through the front door and surprised Bucky Yarborough, who demanded, "What's going on here?"

Kenny managed to squeak out, "Bucky, there was a fella in the bunkhouse who threatened to shoot me. I'm scared to death."

That gun-toting ranch hand was standing outside of the house.

He shrugged and grinned, "I was just funnin' with the new kid."

The boss didn't think it was funny.

He flat told that guy, "Get your gear, you're going to town."

Bucky Yarborough hauled that hand into town, and dumped him off at the railroad station to catch the next freight train to somewhere else."

Kenny finished that first season and earned a man's wage. The pay was $1 per day plus board and room. The next summer, he and his mother repeated their jobs for Bucky Yarborough.

For being a 'punk kid,' as Kenny often referred to himself, "I acquired some important lessons that summer. My mother taught me, 'You have to *learn* to work.'"

"Through being taught to work, I learned how to get along with people and develop a work ethic. A good work ethic was key to making a living. I also learned how to button up my lip and keep on working when necessary, whether I liked it or not."

The benefits of summer ranch work were many. One was being in good shape for school sports in the fall. Others were important lessons in common sense, decency, good reflexes and doing your best. Those experiences shaped Kenny for the rest of his life.

Chapter 12

KENNY'S BASKETBALL GIRLFRIEND

Cora was pleased to have Bud at the University of Wyoming and Kenny at Laramie High School. She had concerns about the social life of her youngest son and wondered why Kenny didn't date or have a girlfriend. Being the president of the Junior class didn't seem to matter much to him. She figured he should take part in additional school activities, such as dances.

When Kenny was pressured to go to a dance, his analysis was, "Mother thought I should participate, for my good. I didn't know much about dancing and I wasn't interested. I just stood around like a dud on the sidelines and held the wall up."

What turned Kenny's crank, however, was sports. He just wanted to play ball. With a laugh, he would describe his girlfriend: "I'd hold my hands out in front of me and make the shape of a basketball. That was my girl. I liked the attention I got in basketball, and girls just didn't fit in."

In exasperation, his mother would complain, "Kenny is only interested in basketball. Basketball-BasketBALL-BASKETBALL!!"

By Kenny's senior year in high school, Cora decided he must go to a dance and dance. With her dogged determination, Kenny's mother reached out to his favorite teacher, who happened to instruct English. She agreed to teach Kenneth to dance.

"The teacher twisted the arm of a classmate of mine to be my partner. Ellen Louise was a nice gal, a very good student, and a decent dancer. I was just not excited about the dance deal.

"My teacher worked hard to get me to move my feet in rhythm with the music. She tried her best to show me how to maneuver my partner around. For cryin' out loud, if I had been on a basketball court, my feet would have danced all over the place."

Not so on the dance floor.

Kenny managed to make it through dance lessons and dances. He couldn't seem to get finished with those pesky social encounters fast enough. Once those requirements were checked off, it was back to where he wanted to be spending his time. In sports.

Being on the hardwood court of the gym with his "girlfriend" brought a spring to his step and determination to his dribbling. His coach, Floyd Forman, was not crazy about the unusual shot that Kenny showed off at times, but he didn't stop him from using it either. This transplant from the farm had the determination to work on the shot which helped him to score on his older brother. When Kenny had to deal with opposing players who were bigger, he would stop on a dime, leap into the air, and release the ball. The tricks he had developed to deal with Bud came in real handy as he faced other players who had the height advantage over him.

Kenny Sailors was noticed by others and he liked the attention. He continued to work on his dribbling, defense, and accuracy. When someone would question Kenny about his unusual shot, the young man always kept a respectful attitude and explained the reason he had come up with such a move. "That's the only way I could shoot over bigger guys."

Key points he developed with his shot were, "Face the basket and square up, be sure to shoot the ball and not just throw it. Remember, it's about the hands, wrists, and fingers."

The ball-handling skills Kenny possessed were not lost on Mr. Foreman.

"Kenny would maneuver defensive players into screens, or direct team members into standing positions so he could move in to score. Kenny was also willing to set others up, so they could go in for the layup."

The spry guard liked to drive into the corner and launch his shot because he didn't have to worry about a defender behind him.

Sailors led the Laramie Plainsmen into two state championship games, in his junior and senior years. A powerful Rock Springs team defeated them the first year. In the second year, the Plainsmen lost to a strong Casper Club by two points. There was some consolation for Kenny. He was selected to the Wyoming All-State High School Basketball Team.

Basketball was not the only high school sport Kenny excelled at. Spring brought out the "thin clads" for the track teams. The broad jump became Kenny's favorite track event and would later be renamed the long jump. He recalled, "As a senior, my longest jump was 19′ 14 1/2.″ A state record at the time. I had strong legs and I loved to jump."

As a senior at the state track meet, Coach Foreman informed Kenny that he was also signed up to run the one-mile event.

"The mile!" Kenny blurted out. "I'd never participated in distance runs before. I did it only to please my coach. Besides, he knew I could run. I had learned about turning on the after-burners during those early morning run and dribble scrimmages in the Hillsdale school gym.

"What do you know? I won the event! My time was four minutes and 48.7 seconds. Good enough to win the championship and beat the guy who was favored to win."

During high school, Kenny lettered in football, basketball, and track and was selected to the All-State High School Football Team for three years.

Kenny remarked, "Classes weren't my biggest priority. Because of that, I had no hope of getting a scholarship offered to me by the university. I wasn't sure how I'd be able to swing the college expenses. With summer jobs, I had some money put away for college, but not enough."

Unexpected opportunities came together to make it possible for the young athlete to enter the University of Wyoming in the fall of 1939.

Chapter 13

COACH EVERETT SHELTON

Kenny knew it would be a stretch to rustle up the money for college expenses. What he didn't realize was his basketball reputation had preceded him. Opportunities arose, to make university life a reality for this scrappy and determined young athlete.

At the beginning of the 1939-40 college term, Kenny enrolled in the University of Wyoming. "I was able to get a job working at 'The Union' cafeteria on campus and the Elks club paid my tuition fees of $50 for my freshman year," Kenny recalled. "I found out later, that Dr. Bass from the Experiment Farm paid other fees for me over the years. This man was an alum of the Phi Delta Theta fraternity. It was through his influence and encouragement that I joined that same fraternity. Greek living wasn't my deal, but I enjoyed making some nice friends."

Through the "Phi Delt" brotherhood, Kenny was paired with an older frat brother, Johnny Winterholler. An outstanding three-sport athlete from Lovell, Wyoming, Johnny became a Marine and was very influential in Kenny's life.

Another bonus for fraternity member Sailors was the timely introduction to an attractive drum majorette and cheerleader from Casper.

Marilynne Corbin would eventually become the wife of Kenneth Sailors.

Kenny needed to declare a major for his college career. His first choice was forestry. "I thought being a forest ranger would be the ticket for me. In those days a ranger led a cowboy life. A cabin was provided for him and his family and they would live out in the forest. I liked the idea of that kind of life. It made me think about the old-time cowboys, Tom Mix and Roy Rogers."

Kenny soon discovered the management and political scene of the Forest Service had shifted from the old days. After his first year of studies, he decided he'd be better off to declare another major and shifted to education, sports, and PE. That change served him well, as years later he was able to teach and coach basketball in Alaska.

Throughout college, Kenny worked at the Student Union in the cafeteria. Dessa Tibbits, the girlfriend of his fraternity big brother Johnny Winterholler, managed the Union.

"I especially appreciated Dessa's pleasant attitude and dedication to everything she did, both at work and in her personal life. She and Johnny were special examples of character and faith to me."

Kenny served meals during dinnertime. In between, he served malts or soft drinks to students at the soda fountain. With his genial personality, integrity, and work ethic, other folks were drawn to him. He did whatever needed to be done.

"Sometimes I'd wait on tables, or clean and scrub the floors. I did it all."

Such visibility contributed to Kenny being voted the most popular man on campus for three years. He never got a big head over the recognition, but continued to reach out and encourage others.

Kenny and teammate Jim Weir worked together at the Student Union. Their pay was twenty-five cents an hour. Kenny added, "Pretty good pay when you consider farm workers were getting one dollar a day. We could also eat any of the food we wanted and I ate all of my meals there. It was good grub."

Kenny recalled, "Mother cooked for fraternity or sorority houses after she sold the boarding house. However, she didn't like staying alone at night, so I went home each evening. I usually walked everywhere that I went."

The fall of 1939 brought a new basketball coach to Laramie to lead the University of Wyoming Cowboys. Born in 1898, Everett Shelton was no rookie. He had grown up on a farm near Cunningham, Kansas, and attended Phillips University in Oklahoma. Shelton coached high school and college ball for some years. His next stint in coaching was in the AAU (Amateur Athletic Union), where he led the Denver Safeways and directed them to an AAU crown in 1937 along with a second-place finish in 1938. During that time, AAU was the best basketball in the country, much bigger than college ball.

"Recruiting players wasn't a deal back then," Kenny acknowledged. On the other hand, Everett Shelton made it his business to learn about potential basketball players coming to the University of Wyoming. He had done his homework where Kenny Sailors was concerned. Ev Shelton soon made himself known to the young fellow.

"Shelton hadn't been in Laramie long when he looked me up," Kenny remembered.

"He said, 'Sailors, they tell me you're going out for football.'"

"I started to tell him how good I was in high school football... He cut mc off."

"I know all about that. You were All-State. I know that. But if you're going to go out for football, just forget about basketball."

"That sort of shocked me. I didn't have anybody I could rely on for advice. I sure couldn't talk to my mother about it."

Kenny thought about his coach at Laramie High and decided he'd pay his former mentor a visit. Floyd Foreman listened to his young friend with a kind ear. After hearing the story of Shelton's ultimatum, Foreman offered up wise words of advice.

He said, "Well you know, Kenny, you only weigh 138 pounds. That's not real heavy for college football."

"I hadn't thought of that. I never got hurt playing high school football. Those guys used to tackle as hard as anyone. I was a punk kid and thought I was tough."

The words of his former coach and mentor started to dawn upon the wannabe college football player.

Kenny saw Coach Foreman sort of turn away from him. Hiding a smile, the older man hesitated. "You know, Kenny, I think I'd listen to him." Kenny Sailors gave Floyd Foreman a measured gaze.

The independent kid decided to follow the advice of this good man, who had his best interests at heart and encouraged him to make hard choices. Each experience with Foreman guided Kenny to become a better person and ball player. Kenny paid attention to Foreman and did not go out for football, but instead looked up Everett Shelton.

Once the basketball die was cast, Kenny knew he had made the right choice.

"Foreman helped me remember how my football career had helped my basketball game. I knew I could adjust to college basketball where the players were bigger and stronger than me. My purpose was to get to the basket. Getting hit hard didn't worry me. And they had a hard time catching me anyway."

Chapter 14

UW BASKETBALL 1939-40

Kenny tried out and was selected for the freshman basketball team at Wyoming.

The rookies had their team schedules, but they worked out and scrimmaged with the varsity team. Varsity teams only included sophomores, juniors, and seniors. Freshmen were not considered eligible in those days.

Coach Shelton made it known to his players that he would like to be called "Ev." They obliged him. He worked to develop solid attributes of character in his players off the court. He was not one bit afraid to roll up his sleeves and go to work with them either. "It was clear to his player's he had standards he wanted upheld no matter where we were. Everett Shelton led the way for his team," said Kenny.

He added, "Shelton became legendary among the teams he shaped because of his dedication to practice and practical advice. Control and discipline were ingrained in him as a coach and transferred seamlessly to teams he guided to success. He was admired for his work ethic, decency, faith, and morals, on and off the court. Shelton lived as an authentic Christian and his life was his witness."

"Tougher than an old boot that Shelton was," said Kenny. "That guy could be tough on his players because of his Marine background. He laid down the rules. Players knew if they broke the rules they'd pay a price. If you played for Shelton, discipline came with the playbook. We knew he cared and that he didn't make idle threats.

"During one practice a teammate and I got into a fistfight. Shelton got the other guy by the hair and me by my neck. He pulled us nose to nose and proceeded to let us have it: 'I don't want to ever—ever, see you fighting again. If you do, you are off the team. Period!'

"Yes, he had our respect alright. We knew he meant business."

Coach Shelton was sort of quiet about his life. When the team learned he had been a Marine in World War I, they were curious about his experiences.

Kenny said, "We found out a few things about him. Shelton had been a machine gunner, involved in trench warfare in Europe. Those guys had to go up and over into one trench from another into no-man's land. Those leathernecks fought in the dark, through barbed wire, and encountered hand-to-hand bayonet fights. He fought his way through the horrific battle of Belleau Woods. My respect and admiration for him grew immensely."

Later on, Shelton would be one of the reasons Kenny joined the Marines. Johnny Winterholler was the other.

Shelton was in lock-step with Cora when it came to discipline and accountability. He drilled into his players that they should always be on the lookout for a sliver of space to cut through: "Dribble. Thread the eye of the needle. Get to the basket."

"That's what I worked on," said Kenny. "Getting to the basket paid off for me, not just in college but also in the pros. My dribble got me past most guys. Especially those fellas that were bigger and slower. I could blow right by 'em. I had some fake moves that helped as well as the jump shot. I also knew driving was important."

When the varsity and freshmen scrimmaged, Kenny and his teammates had a pretty inflated opinion of themselves. Those cocky rookies thought they were hot stuff and didn't hesitate to make that known. Coach Shelton finally had a belly full of their attitude. He decided to take care of the problem.

"You crazy freshman. If you think you can beat the varsity, we'll schedule a game and you can play against them," the coach declared. "Let's see how great you are!"

Kenny spoke for his freshmen teammates: "We knew we could beat them. We played against them every day in practice. I could go past some of them so fast, I'd create a breeze and they'd catch a cold. We were tickled to death when the game was arranged."

The event was scheduled, advertised to the public, and tickets were sold. The "Freshmen vs Varsity" billing drew over four thousand people to attend the match-up—not in the practice Half Acre gym, but in the main auditorium. Newspapers from around the state covered the fascinating event. Not only did the freshmen win, but they beat the varsity soundly, 42-31. Kenny pumped in eleven points. Ev Shelton was surprised. He began to devise a plan on how to shape the two groups into a cooperative unit.

After the game, Kenny and his teammates heard through the grapevine the coach had a change of attitude. Shelton admitted: "I didn't realize those freshmen were such decent ball players. They're pretty good."

Rookies Jim Weir and Kenny worked well together. The next year they were joined by Floyd Volker and Lew Roney. These four players, products of Wyoming high schools, went on to be at the core of Cowboy basketball for the next four years.

Another star player for the Cowboys was a couple of years older than Kenny. Curt Gowdy of Green River, Wyoming, was a five-foot-nine guard who had been a three-year varsity letterman in basketball and tennis for the university.

Gowdy and Sailors were competitors for the starting line-up on the basketball team as well as the dating game. Kenny wound up dating the girl Curt had been dating before she met Kenny. Marilynne

Corbin eventually became the bride of Sailors. Gowdy went on to a storied career as the very popular and well-known national sportscaster and host of a sports program of his own, Wyoming Outdoors.

While Gowdy and Sailors played together, they weren't particularly close. Gowdy later described Kenny as among the best he'd ever seen play on the hardwood. "He was a great dribbler and very, very quick. He struck like a rattlesnake. His speed was the main thing I remember about him. He was a good shot and spectacular to watch."

Everett Shelton made it clear to the Wyoming players that while he had earned an AAU championship, he had a dream of a national college basketball championship. Sailors and Weir on his freshman team would become a nucleus to make that dream a reality.

A reality that Kenny didn't have to dream about was the support of his mother. Since the family now lived in town, Cora had the luxury of some free time. When the Cowboys played in the Hell's Half Acre gym, she could be found perched in the balcony above the basketball floor watching. She sat still, without emotion. But she was there. She was there.

Kenny would glance up and see her. He said, "Mother told me she would keep scrapbooks of my basketball activities. But, she didn't want me looking through the newspapers to read about myself. I guess it was another way for her to keep me humble."

The basketball season of 1939-40 was not a great year for the varsity Cowboys and their new coach. Freshman games were difficult to schedule because colleges did not want to spend money on that part of the program. Kenny added, "We didn't have much competition. Each team we played, we beat badly. Opposing schools didn't want to come to Laramie anyway."

At 7,200 feet, the altitude was intimidating. The record for Shelton's first varsity season was a lackluster 6-10. After the freshman boys upset the varsity, the coach developed a plan to get the Cowboys turned around. He had the young talent to win for the next few years

Chapter 15

UW BASKETBALL 1940-41

With the enthusiasm and prowess of the now sophomore varsity players, the 1940-41 Cowboys' season ended on a better note with fourteen wins and six losses. Of those twenty games, only seven were at home. The home conference games scheduled for the Pokes had to be played on the Half Acre gym court in Laramie. Colorado didn't like to play in the Half Acre gym because the fans were rowdy. People crowded onto chairs courtside and on a balcony that overlooked the floor. It was an intimidating venue to play in.

Kenny commented, "Colorado cried their eyes out when they had to come play. Coach Frosty Cox hated the Half Acre gym. They tried to make all kinds of deals with us to play on a neutral court. Shelton would not allow that of course."

Shelton began to bump the ante up. He scheduled non-conference games with any tough teams in the surrounding area that would be willing to host the Wyoming team. His strategy was developed to make his team the best they could be. The games were played on the opponent's home court and the cowboys made the trek by train or bus. Often Shelton would be the bus driver. With an average of 7.3

points per game, Kenny went on to win his first letter in varsity basketball.

The second-year coach brought a clever offense to college basketball. He had developed a methodical maneuver, dubbed the "Shelton Weave." The Cowboys learned to work the play to perfection. Whether setting very important screens or making drives, each player was in constant motion. This action was effective in setting up an outside shooter or allowing for another to drive inside for a short shot, or an easy layup.

"There wasn't any defense against that offense at the time," Kenny said.

Coach Shelton was adamant his players develop a winning mentality and never expect to lose.

He continued to harp on his team: "Don't worry about playing on the road. All the courts are regulation size. The baskets are all the same height and the basketballs are the same size. The number of players is the same. Everything is the same."

Each detail was hashed and rehashed for team members to digest. The only thing different at away games was the crowd's attitude.

Kenny recalled, "At home, people cheered for you. Away from home, the crowd would boo you." One of Shelton's favorite sayings was, "They won't boo a bum. People might boo, but they will recognize a good team when they see one."

The solution was to become a great player. Do your job. Be a person of determination. Kenny knew he sure wasn't a bum. "But, I never forgot that statement."

One thing Coach Shelton was not in favor of was weightlifting.

He'd say, "I don't want a bunch of muscle-bound basketball players running around."

Kenny remembered, "Coach's idea of conditioning came through loud and clear. RUN. We ran and ran and ran in practice. Are you kidding me?"

Back in those days, weight training was frowned upon.

"On the other hand, Shelton had an idea for staying in shape," Kenny said. "He set me and Jimmy Reese up with summer jobs, working ten-hour shifts at the Monolith Portland Midwest Cement Company. We were stationed at the end of a conveyor belt with 100-pound bags of dry cement being dropped in front of us. We'd grab the bags, haul them to a waiting railroad box car, and stack them. Run-stack-repeat. Believe me, we were on the trot.

"Talk about getting conditioned! We did, and built upper body strength as a benefit.

"Smart guy, that Everett Shelton."

After a day of hoisting cement bags, Kenny and Jimmy would go to the gym on campus.

"Coach Shelton had given me a key to unlock the door. We'd scrimmage one-on-one and he expected us to keep a record of who won. Coach always had a competition of some sort. Next, we'd set up dozens of chairs to create an obstacle course on the floor of the court and dribble through the maze to improve our speed and ball handling."

Something more serious was on Kenny's mind as he worked and practiced. Bud had quit college and joined the Army Air Corps in 1941. Due to the absence of their father, Kenny had looked up to and leaned on his brother, through all of his growing-up years. Now that Bud was gone, this new coach began to fill a void in Kenny's life.

Kenny appreciated Everett Shelton.

"Ev became a role model and mentor to me. His guidance stuck with me throughout life and I made the most of any opportunity to credit Shelton for all he poured into me."

The plucky shooter from Hillsdale paid close attention to what his advisor had to offer the Cowboys. Shelton's presence added stability to Kenny's world. A world that had changed dramatically because of the ongoing war.

When Shelton spoke, Kenny listened.

Ev would expound, "If we're ever gonna make the big time, we gotta play big-time teams. We gotta go to New York and the East Coast because that's where the publicity and the celebrity teams are."

Coach Shelton realized he had to get his small-time school into upper-level venues. Wyoming began to gain notoriety as they traveled east to play Georgetown, Canisius, Long Island, St. John's, CCNY, and others. Game by game, the University of Wyoming Cowboys showed they had what it took to be a part of big-time play.

In March of 1941, the Pokes earned a berth in the Western Regionals of the Third Annual NCAA tournament. A top-rated Arkansas organization featuring Johnny Adams tripped them up in their first game and defeated them. Creighton outlasted the Cowboys in the consolation game, squeaking out a one-point victory.

Although he was in a losing cause, Kenny Sailors was declared the hero of the day. The news outlets could not say enough about how a spindly-legged sophomore on the Wyoming bench at the start of the contest, entered the fray and won the crowd.

Kenny had listened well to Ev Shelton: "If you want to drive to the hoop, Sailors, don't pussy-foot around a guy."

"Coach went on to show me how to knock a defender off balance and continue a slashing drive. I worked on that move and continued to refine my shot."

His play and execution worked for him. Shelton allowed him, even encouraged him, to use his shot. Thanks to Bud, the big bum of a brother, he had an effective way to get around taller, defensive players.

Chapter 16

CORA PUTS HER FOOT DOWN

"You think you'd like to go where and do what?" Cora Sailors gave her youngest son Kenneth a penetrating look. The light glinted off the glasses perched on her nose. She paused for emphasis. "Where did you get such an idea?"

Kenny swallowed before answering. "You see Mother, after we played the Utah Redskins on their home court in Salt Lake City, their coach, Vadal Peterson, had a little talk with my friend Jim Weir. Peterson said he'd offer us scholarships if we would transfer to Utah to play for them. He told us we could have more playing time and maybe even have a chance to start."

Cora glared as Kenny squirmed in the front room of their home.

In February of 1941, Kenny and Jim were both Sophomores at UW. Kenny liked to describe himself and his basketball buddies as punk kids. He and Jim were the same age and had both been All-State players in high school. The two young men figured they were pretty hot stuff when they were selected for the University of Wyoming junior varsity team as freshmen. The fact that they beat the varsity team in a highly publicized game, only added to their cocky attitude.

Coach Shelton tried to quash the behavior of his younger players by giving them a generous dose of time on the bench, out of play, thinking about how they might change their attitudes. Instead, Sailors and Weir counted how many minutes of play they didn't get.

When Jim told Kenny about the Utah offer, the two friends gave serious thought to transferring to the neighboring state. That is until Kenny mentioned the opportunity to his mother.

"We'll just see about that Kenneth," His mother put on her hat, grabbed her purse, and headed out the door.

Kenny groaned. Whenever his mother called him Kenneth, it was not a good sign.

Cora made her way to the office of the university president to see him about a matter of concern.

Mrs. Sailors gave the president the lowdown on the out-of-state offer that had been given to her son and Jim Weir.

The light glinted off of Cora's glasses. Kenneth's mother looked the distinguished gentleman in the eye and stated: "I just need to tell you, sir, that my son will not be transferring to Utah. He will stay in Wyoming to complete his education and remain playing for the Cowboys. Period."

When Cora returned home, she sat her son down and gave him the news.

"I'm putting my foot down Kenneth, you are not going anywhere. You'll stay here and finish what you started."

She did. He did. Jim Weir did too. And the rest is history.

To use a phrase that Bill Schrage, a sports historian, coined: "Kenny's mother could go down in Wyoming history as the 'unheralded heroine' of Cowboy basketball. Without Kenny Sailors and Jim Weir, Wyoming would likely never have made it to the court of Madison Square Garden and a national basketball championship."

Chapter 17

UW BASKETBALL 1941-42

Coach Everett Shelton wanted to allow his motivated Cowboys to play against better teams. "Ev got us all together and explained his plan," Kenny recalled.

"Lookey," Shelton said. "We'll never win a championship playing second-rate teams. It can't be done. You've got to play the best opponents."

Basketball teams on the East Coast in the early 1940s had no desire to come to the Wyoming high plains to play exhibition games. Shelton went to work with his athletic director to schedule games with stronger teams. An on-the-road calendar was soon filled. The cross-country train trip was scheduled and the Cowboys were on the move.

Kenny continued, "We made long train trips: Rochester, Philadelphia, New York City. We slept in Pullman berths on the trains. Those short beds were rough on the big guys with long legs. The only place for their feet was out in the aisle. The coach told them to get as much rest as they could despite the space.

"Shelton had our trips planned. He made sure we were in good physical shape, took in educational sights along the way, and kept up with our studies.

“I’ve told the story about an English paper I didn’t get turned in.

Coach Shelton made it a point to check on the academic progress of his team three times a week when we were on campus. One week he checked with my English teacher and she said I was missing a paper.

“Shelton immediately came to me. We were supposed to head to New York City the next Monday on the train. The first comment he made to me was, ‘Kenny, you’re not planning on going to New York with us.’ He didn’t say, ‘I’m not taking you.’ Just, ‘You’re not planning on going with us to New York.’

“Well, I was counting on going, Coach. Is there some reason?”

“There’s a good reason. You have an English paper due. Make sure you get it to your teacher. If you don’t have it in, you won’t be boarding the train.”

Kenny laughed. “Guess what? I finished the paper and handed it in on time.”

“Shelton demanded we take our books on all of our trips. Our teachers prepared assignments for us to work on while we traveled. Coach made sure we had a space to complete our lessons. There was no question about it. We’d better do the work. Period.”

The Cowboys landed in New York City for Christmas of 1941. “The hustle and bustle of the big city was a marvel. For some reason, it was not as overwhelming as I thought it might be. Here I was a country kid, but I didn’t go clear off my rocker. I handled it alright I guess.”

“New York City was a fascinating town, but the attitudes I encountered made me realize I wouldn’t want to live there. It was an interesting experience, to say the least.”

Shelton connected with Madison Square Garden promoter Ned Irish to advance his Cowboy team.

“Once we hit the ‘Big Apple,’ Mr. Ned Irish had us decked out in cowboy hats, shirts, and boots to gain some attention for our upcoming event at the Garden. That did the trick. People did notice us, but they wondered if we Cowboys from the west even knew what a basket was.”

Shelton wanted his boys to take in some of the culture of the city and Ned Irish was happy to make sure that happened. He rounded up tickets for high society events for the Wyoming players to enjoy.

"Jim Weir and I decided we would attend a performance at the Metropolitan Opera. Ned Irish directed us to wear our cowboy duds to attend the event, and we were happy to oblige him. When we walked into the very formal, black-tie affair, more than one eyebrow was raised as we politely walked in to find our seats. We enjoyed the high-brow musical presentation but found ourselves singing *Home on the Range* as we returned to our hotel.

Irish was correct. We did rustle up some interest in the Cowboys from the high plains who would be playing at the famous Madison Square Garden."

The day arrived for the first game to be played. When it came time for pre-game activities in the Garden arena, the country kids from Laramie were staggered by the introductions. Kenny spoke for the other players when he said, "I couldn't believe it. All the lights were shut off. A spotlight came on as a player ran onto the floor. Our name was announced. Here we were, a bunch of kids just off the farm. I'd never before experienced anything like that. It was pretty heady stuff."

Those guys from small-town America did not let the spotlight go to their heads. They were there on a mission.

Kenny offered a little background on the way games were played in those years.

"Coaches were not allowed on the floor like they are today."

Everett Shelton had no problem with that idea. His thought was, "Have your coaching done before you get onto the court. The players should be able to take it from there."

The Wyoming ball players received that message early on. Shelton was as direct as he was charming. Alan Simpson, a former Cowboy player who lettered in 1953 and went on to become a United States Senator from Wyoming, had a comical recollection about Shelton making his point.

"The coach wouldn't curse, but led by example. He had our respect and we believed in him. Shelton drilled us hard in practice. He was not above getting in our face to make an emphatic point. He'd give us a thump on our forehead with his finger and say, 'Did you hear what I said?' He didn't have to shout at you. Only look. When we got the look, there was no messing around. We got the point, believe me."

Simpson chuckled as he rubbed a spot on his forehead—a reminder of where Shelton had impressed his point below Alan's hairline. It was obvious that Sailors and other Cowboy players had gotten the look and received a thump from their coach as well. They all paid attention.

"When we prepared to begin our first game at the Garden, Shelton knew he could depend on his captain and team members to do what he'd taught them. He figured the antics of some coaches running around and yelling on the sidelines was a bunch of bunk. Anyway, the rules prohibited that type of behavior. He had confidence in his boys. He knew we would get the job done."

The team had come together into a tight-knit group. While there were no trophies, the University of Wyoming Cowboys had gained national attention and finished the season with a respectable 15-5 record after beating CCNY at Madison Square Gardens. Kenny was named an All-Conference player.

Everett Shelton and his team looked forward to what the next basketball season would bring their way, even while many of the boys were thinking about a call to serve their country through military service.

Chapter 18

1942-43 UW CHAMPIONSHIP TEAM

The University of Wyoming basketball team started the 1942-43 season with a preseason road trip to Georges Island in Massachusetts. During the war, military bases were stacked with good players. On December 11, the Pokes played Fort Warren in a doubleheader. The team came out of the chute to win the first game 49-33, and ended up with a 53-43 win in the second encounter. One week later, Wyoming defeated the Fort Warren All-Stars 63-40.

After that tour, The Pokes encountered a wake-up call in their first game with another big-name team: Duquesnc in Pittsburg.

Charles "Chick" Davies, the coach at Duquesne, scheduled the contest at a court of his choice. He chose a small cage-type venue, surrounded by fences, commonly referred to as a "cracker box." The crowded and unfamiliar playing venue shut down the Wyoming offense.

Kenny recalled the game, "We were not used to a small gym with close quarters and were not able to make the necessary corrections. I was stymied and could not drive as I typically did."

The Cowboys were shaken up by the 43-33 loss, the only defeat they suffered at the hands of a college team that year.

Shelton stated, "No sense in complaining." He made needed adjustments and the team paid attention. The boys learned from their defeat. The Pokes went on to win the next twenty-three games in a row.

During the St. Francis game in Brooklyn, Sailors had 17 points. Jim Weir added 18 points, and center Milo Komenich scored 21 points in the tally. The final score of 63-38, and a 25-point margin, made the bigshots sit up and take notice. The newspaper writers of the Big Apple were impressed.

Returning home after Christmas, the Cowboys had an 8-1 record. Other wins on the road swing were: Albright College, 56-52 in Reading, Pennsylvania; LaSalle, 56-32 in Philadelphia; St. Francis of Pennsylvania at Madison Square Gardens in New York City, 63-38; in upstate New York, Rochester 68-44; and to Southfield, Michigan, to polish off Lawrence Tech, 78-34.

Most of these teams were not highly regarded, but St. Francis had come into the contest with a 6-0 record. Rochester hadn't lost a home game in two seasons.

Shelton had a stark reminder for his team as they came in from seeing some of the New York City sights: "Lookey boys, if you keep your heads screwed on straight, you can beat anybody."

Wyoming won the conference championship, beating Utah twice, CSU twice, and BYU three times. They twice defeated the eventual AAU champions, Phillips 66, in two, one-point games. In one of those games, Kenny's dribbling skills were spotlighted. Shelton said, "As Kenny dribbled out the clock, no one could stop him. He kept the ball for one minute and twenty-six seconds."

After finishing third in the national AAU tournament and losing their only other game to Denver Legion, Kenny was named to the First Team AAU All-Americans. The Pokes then returned to college ball, defeating Oklahoma 53-50 and Texas 58-53 in the NCAA regionals in Kansas City.

The NCAA title game between Georgetown and Wyoming ended up in a nail-biting barn burner where the teams went neck and neck. At halftime, the score was only 18-16. The score was tied five times in the first half … and five times in the second half.

From the beginning of the event on that famous New York City court, Wyoming showed just what they were made of. Sailors continued driving to the basket. Georgetown was able to slow the game down slightly. Kenny pumped in 16 points, the high for his team. The scrappy boy who first jumped in front of a windmill made a big impression on teams and spectators alike with his unusual shot. The Hoyas moved out a 31-26 lead.

The Pokes continued to play controlled ball and threw in an occasional fast break as they effectively moved forward under the cool guidance of Kenny Sailors. The unbelievable was about to happen. In the final moments of the match, the game turned into a rout.

The University of Wyoming 1943 Championship team.
Kenny standing to the right of the trophy and coach Everett Shelton.
(Photo courtesy of Sailors family.)

It was mayhem as the clock ran down and the highly touted NCAA National Championship game ended. The score was 46-34!

That game was a watershed event for Kenny and jettisoned him into the national sports spotlight. He was voted the "Most Outstanding Player" for the whole tournament.

The Cowpokes reacted with control and class. "When the game ended, we didn't do much shouting or jumping," Kenny said. Shelton wouldn't tolerate any of that emotional stuff. He just patted me on the back and said, 'Nice game. Nice game.' That was about it. We were all happy, but we didn't get silly. Not on the court. But in the locker room, we whacked each other on the back a bit. Shelton was all smiles, but kept us in line."

Quickly a battle for bragging rights developed over who was the best team in the country.

St. John's of New York had won the NIT (National Invitation Tournament). They were the "kings" of the city. Ken recounted, "Shelton felt the New York City newspapers did not give Wyoming the credit they deserved for winning the NCAA championship. They were working us over in the papers, saying the NCAA was the newcomer and not in the same standing as the NIT."

Kenny continued, "Ev Shelton went to promoter Ned Irish with the idea of a national playoff game between the NCAA winner and the NIT winner. Irish immediately grabbed the opportunity and ran with it. An event was set up in two days to settle the issue of who the best team in the nation was. The match-up was to be a fundraiser for the American Red Cross. With over 18,000 spectators in attendance, the event provided $26,000 for the relief organization."

It had been predicted the game would be a fitting end to the college season, and it surely was. The teams were evenly matched. With a controversial foul and a questionable call, at the end of regulation play, the score was tied. In the overtime session, Wyoming outlasted St. John's, 52-47. The question of a mythical national title was settled. One expert left the Garden the night of April 1 exclaiming, "Sailors is just out of this world." He scored only 11 points, but his real impact came through his dribbling and directing skills as team captain. The many awards he received included "NCAA Most Valuable Tournament Player" and being selected as an "All-American."

Once the celebration died down, the Cowboys were met by the Washington-based politicians of Wyoming at their Manhattan hotel. Kenny described it as "The big feed. Lots of food, important people, and a pretty gal set up for each basketball player, to talk with. Nothing more."

Pictures were taken with the players and women sitting next to each other. Kenny was engaged to a special young woman back home. He said, "When my girlfriend saw a picture of that deal, she didn't like it." Kenny reflected, "In the six games I played in Madison Square Garden, I was not on a losing team."

There was a sense of pride and satisfaction in the group when the Cowboys boarded the train for Wyoming. However, the war issue loomed before them all. Times were unsettled after the bombing of Pearl Harbor. Some students immediately enlisted, leaving behind whatever families and activities they were involved in. Others waited for the draft.

Kenny said, "This was an era of high patriotism in our country. Young men were willing to serve and eager to get to war. Even the not-so young men were willing to serve. I learned that my former high school coach Floyd Foreman had enlisted and was involved in the rigorous physical training of young recruits. I'd always thought a lot of him. Now I appreciated him even more. I was lucky he was a mentor at a time when I had no father to guide me during impressionable years. God was always looking out for me."

Sailors had joined the ROTC program when he entered the University. His mentors Johnny Winterholler and Ev Shelton had influenced his decision to join the Marines.

Kenny was committed to his fiancé, and events would move forward quickly. He had a national basketball championship and numerous awards to his credit. Kenny would be married in the summer and a Marine prepared to serve in World War II by that autumn.

Before leaving Laramie for Quantico on April 9, 1943, Kenny went to the movies at the Fox Theatre in Laramie. He was surprised and pleased to see the *Movietonews* preview showing the Wyoming Cowboys playing in the "mythical national championship game." Three days later, he was on his way to officer training.

Chapter 19

REAL LIVE GIRLFRIEND

Kenny had been perfectly happy with the convenient basketball which had substituted for a girlfriend. The ball had been a steady companion during his high school and early college years. In the fall of 1942, his friend Stan Hathaway cornered Kenny at his job as a soda jerk, where he also waited tables in the Union.

Stan and Kenny had known each other through high school sports. They joked how they "were both poor as church mice." Stan cleaned the house for the Kappa sorority. He told Kenny, "You should be waiting tables at the Kappa Gamma house instead of the Student Union. We've got some really cute girls from Casper over there. You ought to meet some of them."

"Well," Kenny said. "Why are you keeping them all for yourself? Bring 'em in here sometime and get us introduced."

Stan returned a few days later with not one but four nice-looking sorority sisters. Kenny was pleasantly surprised. The last gal to be introduced was Marilynne Corbin.

"I recognized her as a cheerleader and the drum majorette," Kenny said. "She's the one that threw the baton thing up in the air when the band marched." Kenny figured Stan must have been talking to her beforehand about his dislike of dances. In the slang of that era, he could have been called a "dead hoofer."

"Kenny, I think you should ask Marilynne to go to the Phi Delta Theta fraternity dance that's coming up," Stan said.

"I don't like to dance much and I'm not a very good dancer," Kenny mumbled.

"Marilynne," Stan said, "You told me you don't dance a whole lot and don't care about it."

Stan the matchmaker was hard at work trying to get Kenny a date. He had sort of asked Marilynne to go to the frat dance with Kenny earlier.

Marilynne smiled at Kenny and said, "Well I don't like to dance much myself."

Stan groaned.

Finally, the deal was made. The pair who said they didn't dance much went to the fraternity dance and…didn't dance much. They did have a good time talking and enjoyed the company of others. They even partook of the refreshment table.

The next week Marilynne decided to reciprocate.

"Kenny, I know you don't like to dance much and I don't like to dance much, but would you like to go to my sorority dance?"

"How could I refuse an offer like that," Kenny said. "Sure, I'll go with you." They went to the dance and…didn't dance much. They did keep talking. Thus began a nearly 60-year relationship of friendship, marriage, parenting, and faith.

"We hit it right off," Mr. Non-Dancer said. "We had a great time talking. She was athletic and liked to hunt and fish. It was nice to find out how much we had in common."

Marilynne laughed as she recalled their first date. "We went fishing. I went upstream. He went downstream. That way there was no 'hanky panky' going on. On a lot of our dates we went fishing and always competed to see who would catch the most fish. We hiked in the hills around town and often took a picnic lunch with us. Sometimes we stayed at the Kappa sorority house and just talked."

"By sitting and talking," Kenny added, "I learned that Marilynne had an unusual nickname: Boky."

When asked how she ended up with that "handle," Boky told him a story about her father, B.H. Corbin.

Marilynne said, "When I was little, Dad had a smoking stand next to his chair. On the stand was a cute wooden decoration attached by a spring. I loved to give the piece a twang and watch the thing jiggle back and forth and say, "boke." I didn't speak very clearly and my dad thought I was trying to say smoke. He started calling me Boky and it stuck."

Both Kenny and Marilynne had a good sense of humor and enjoyed a good laugh whenever they spent time together.

Marilynne had a twinkle in her eye as she looked at Kenny one day.

"Yes, I think it's the color of corn tassels."

Kenny craned his head, raised his eyebrows, and looked Marilynne in the eye.

"What are you talking about now? We were just discussing horses."

The perky girl tossed her head and restated. "I think your hair is the color of corn tassels in ripe field corn. Besides, the way your hair stands up it looks sort of like a corn shock. Corn tassel and corn shock. Sort of goes together, don't you think?"

Kenny rolled his eyes and scratched his shock of hair.

Boky continued, "You know my nickname and now I have one for you. How about that?"

Kenny paused, "I've spent plenty of time in the corn fields with horses pulling a wagon. Now let's get to the main topic of our discussion. Horses."

"Fine with me, Corn tassel," laughed Boky.

"Corn tassel," chuckled Kenny. "Time to apply some horse sense to this conversation."

"If we could find someone to let us borrow horses to ride, we'd do that. Marilynne liked all of the outdoor stuff. At first, I thought she was kidding me, but she enjoyed it all. Boky had grown up in a rural area and had learned to shoot at an early age. She was like my mother, who could shoot the head right off a chicken."

"Some of the outdoor discussions we had included Alaska, or The Last Frontier as the territory was nicknamed. We were always fascinated with Alaska and very attracted to the place."

Kenny said of Boky, "She was not only good-looking, but I noticed the inner beauty she had as well. We seemed to 'click' from the start and spent most of our free time together."

Early in the year of 1943, Kenny asked Marilynne to marry him. No surprise, she accepted.

Kenny would remark many times: "Those two women, my wife and mother, had more influence on my whole life than any other two people. Both women were down-to-earth commonsense kind of gals who liked the outdoors."

.....

In mid-April 1943, after Kenny and the team returned from New York City activities, the winter quarter of college finished. Like other universities in the country during wartime, the University of Wyoming conferred degrees upon senior students who were nearing graduation. Kenny received a degree in Education even though he was eight credits short of the requirements. Sailors would soon leave for training.

"I already had my commission because I was one of the top leaders in the Wyoming ROTC (Reserve Officers' Training Corps) program," Sailors said. "I received the same type of recognition as Johnny Winterholler, my big brother in the fraternity. The Marines gave a permanent second lieutenant commission to one successful person in the ROTC unit. Both of us were so honored."

The rigorous life Kenny had led growing up on a hard-scrabble farm and in the sports arena contributed to the discipline and determination that moved him into military leadership.

The training at Quantico was administered by NCOs (Non-Commissioned Officers). Kenny said, "Those guys didn't mess around. I learned very quickly to pay attention, listen to what they said, and *do* as they said. Period."

"I had grown up in a disciplined environment, so this training wasn't as tough on me as it was on some of the other guys. Some of the recruits couldn't make it and washed out. I didn't."

"When the training was finished in July," Kenny said, "I headed back home on a ten-day pass. I would then continue to the Marine base in San Diego, California. In the orders I received, I was told specifically not to bring any family members with me. There was no room to house them on base."

"I headed to northwest Wyoming to the town of Frannie, where Marilynne was staying with her mother Sallie. When I arrived, she and I had to figure out what our next steps would be. Our parents counseled us to wait before we made plans. They recognized the dire consequences of war."

Marilynne had a flat statement. "I'm going with you. We're engaged and we'll be married. Period."

Chapter 20

MARILYNNE AND MARRIAGE

"Marilynne was not fazed by the thought of her husband not returning from combat," Kenny recalled. "I had come to grips with the fact I might not come home."

"We had a short visit with Sallie, a messenger for the Union Pacific Railroad in the remote town. Her mother took us to the station to board the eastbound train for Chadron, Nebraska, where her father, B.H. Corbin, was the Union Pacific station manager. Mr. Corbin picked us up and let us know right off the bat he didn't think we should marry either. The chance his daughter would become a war widow was high. However, Marilynne was adamant."

Mr. Corbin had been notified about the possible marriage and had made plans for a quiet ceremony in Chadron. Just in the event...

Kenny continued, "Her dad took us to the courthouse and guided us down a hallway to an office where a man sitting behind a desk was all smiles. Turned out he was B.H.'s friend—the local dogcatcher! I was to learn that both of these guys had quite a sense of humor."

"Her dad didn't leave us in a muddle for too long and told us what the 'Plan B' was. He invited us to follow him to his church, where the pastor then married us. It was July 8, 1943."

Mr. & Mrs. Kenny Sailors married July 8, 1943, in Chadron, Nebraska. Photo by B.H. Corbin, father of Marilynne. (Courtesy of Sailors family.)

The new Mr. and Mrs. Sailors took a train to California, and during the trip they met another couple in the same situation. The young man was also a Marine and not supposed to bring a wife. He, too, was aware of all the restrictions involving families.

There were a few days before the men had to report to the base. The group put their four heads together and devised a plan. The quartet bought pillows, blankets, and a bit of food before heading to a local park.

Kenny continued, "We found benches to sleep on at night and wandered around during the day while looking for rooms to rent. Our friends found a room fairly quickly and let us know there was a closet large enough for us to squeeze in a three-quarter-sized bed if we wanted to bunk with them. We rustled up a bed and moved off the park benches on the third day."

The fellows had to report for duty. Marilynne continued to look for a place where she could stay long-term. In a chance encounter,

Boky met a woman named Mrs. Bahu who was willing to discuss the possibility of renting her a room.

The Bahu family were Christians who had to flee from Palestine because of their faith. Mrs. Bahu and Marilynne connected immediately. The young bride was invited to come live with the family which included two teenage sons. Marilynne introduced Kenny to the family later that day. The Bahus kindly invited him to join them for the evening meal.

"I was surprised," said Kenny. "Those folks were so nice to Boky and me. Mrs. Bahu said, 'Please come to have meals with us when you can.' I did and it was the beginning of a wonderful relationship. Mrs. Bahu had a tremendous influence on Marilynne, guiding her to accept Jesus Christ as her Savior."

"I knew Marilynne was a wonderful person, but coming to know the Lord made a big difference in her life and our marriage. Over the several months Marilynne lived with those folks, Mrs. Bahu discipled her and helped her grow in her Christian life. Marilynne's new faith would have an impact on me too."

When Kenny shipped out in early 1944, Marilynne was pregnant with their first child and stayed with the Bahus for a few more weeks. They had become good friends and remained in touch through the years.

After the dust settled, Marilynne returned to Laramie to stay with Kenny's mother and resume studies at the University.

"Staying with Kenny's mother was good for both of us," said Marilynne. "Cora and I got along well."

"On September 30, 1944, our baby Linda Jean was born in Laramie. I wrote a letter to Kenny to let him know he had a daughter."

In the spring of 1945, Marilynne had been notified Kenny would be arriving in San Francisco, California, for a brief stop-over. She wasn't about to miss the chance to see her husband and introduce his baby girl to him.

Marilynne and infant traveled by train to San Francisco to be present for the arrival of Kenny's ship. To her dismay, she learned there were no hotel rooms available. She put on "her thinking cap" and best smile. Packing her darling daughter, a determined Mrs. Sailors began to call on the finest hotels in the city.

This charming woman entered the lobby of the impressive St. Francis Hotel and asked to speak to the manager. She stated her case. "Sir, my husband will soon be docking on the *U.S.S. Robert E Callan.* He is a Marine Lieutenant who has been on duty in the South Pacific for the past eighteen months. I have been unable to find a room for us. It's time he met his new daughter. Is there any way you might help me out?"

It didn't take long for the manager to find a room for the family. When the time arrived for Kenny's ship to dock, Marilynne and the baby took a taxi to meet her husband.

The long-awaited reunion came when Marilynne finally saw Kenny walking down the gangplank. Jostling her way through the exuberant throng, she was finally swept up in the embrace of her husband. Baby Linda squirmed through all the hullabaloo.

Moving away from the undulating mass of humanity, Kenny asked his wife, "Where are you staying? We probably can't find a park bench for the baby."

She grinned at him and stated, "I've got a surprise for you Corn Tassel."

When the family of three made their way to the deluxe hotel, Kenny looked at her in shock.

"What's going on here? We can't afford this can we?"

With delight, Marilynne laughed and told her story. "After I spoke with the manager and told him who you were, he said they would ensure we were taken care of. Let's go inside."

Kenny was dumbfounded. "The manager of the St. Francis Hotel took us up to the fancy Bridal Suite. In one of the rooms was a large dresser with drawers big enough to make a bed for the baby. We had everything you could imagine for our stay. I could not believe it!"

The brief time the Sailors family had in the Golden Gate City was unforgettable. All too soon they had to say goodbye at the dock. Kenny was shipped out west for the Pacific, and the girls headed east to Wyoming. "What a time we had together. To think my wife was able to work out such a deal.

"That was something."

Marilynne was thankful for all she had learned from her friend Mrs. Bahu about the power of prayer and trust in the living God.

.....

The rest of that story.

In 2008, Kenny journeyed to San Diego, California, from Wyoming with his nephew Dale Sailors.

"I had planned and found the contact information for the Bahus in Marilynne's address book. I'd written to the Bahu boys earlier to let them know I was coming to town and would like to visit them. We made plans to meet at the family home. Dale used that locator contraption thing in his car (aka known as GPS), to find out how to get to the Bahu residence. By golly, we drove right to the place.

"The old folks were gone, but both sons were there to greet us. The boys and I recognized each other immediately, even though it had been decades since we were last together. It was a wonderful time of reunion. God surely had His hand on all of us over the years."

Chapter 21

MARINE CORPS

When Kenny first arrived at the Marine Corps Amphibious Training Base in 1943, he received quite an education from the NCOs. Those instructors wasted no time in informing the rookies what was expected of a Marine officer. Coach Shelton had commented years before: "Athletes make good soldiers. They have learned the importance of discipline, character, executing a plan, and teamwork."

Yes indeed.

The Marines stationed in Coronado cobbled together a basketball team led by Kenny Sailors of Wyoming and Joe Fulks of Murray State in Kentucky. Sailors and Fulks had both received credit for developing jump shots. With former Wyoming standouts, Floyd Volker and Jimmy Collins, the leathernecks had one of the most powerful Armed Forces basketball teams in the country.

The leathernecks and their teammates faced off with other top military basketball players. In 1943-44, Sailors and Fulks were able to introduce other servicemen to their innovative jump shots.

Various writers throughout the country described the military as a mixing bowl of basketball styles. One former "anchor clacker" and basketball player of that era stated: "The first time I saw a jump shot I was in the Navy stationed in Hawaii. We had this interservices squad and played a team from the West Coast. Man, those guys were jumping high off the court into the air. We didn't know what the heck to do."

Basketball became one small way for servicemen to let off some steam and focus on teamwork before they were deployed. Those basketball forays may have even led to activities that resulted in the creation of the "Military Basketball Association," or MBA in 2017.

In those months, the Marines faced tough sledding with other teams. The college squads, industrial league teams, and AAU players were no pushovers. The leathernecks gained a name for themselves and were undefeated in 35 games. The military basketball play could have been a way to spread the use of the jump shot, after the war.

When a change of command occurred at the San Diego base, the incoming three-star general made a statement to the area newspa-

Second Lt. Kenny Sailors with Marine security detail on board the U.S.S. General Robert E. Callan. 1944. (Courtesy Sailors family.)

pers. "What are we doing? Are we fighting a war or are we playing basketball?"

It was a wake-up call for the Marine team when the news got out the general had lost a son on Tarawa in the Pacific. That sobering statement from a grieving father placed sports in a completely different context.

Kenny said, "Within three weeks I was out on a transport ship, the *U.S.S. General Robert E. Callan,* headed to the Pacific. On the ship, I was in charge of a 40 to 50-man security detail. We carried black troop replacements to the South Pacific Islands such as Guam and Saipan. Troop ships were a prime candidate for enemy submarines.

"I knew my brother Bud was flying B-25s somewhere in the Pacific, but didn't know where. We were both a long way from the dirt corral of Hillsdale, Wyoming."

Kenny made a poignant statement. "There always was some guilt I dealt with because I was the NCAA Most Valuable Player and an All-American. I wondered if the Marines weren't a little careful about where they sent me. I lost a lot of friends. My fraternity big brother, Johnny Winterholler, survived the 'Death March of Bataan' in the Philippines. He was beaten so badly he ended up losing both of his legs when he returned home.

"After the war I learned his fiancé Dessa, from the Union days back in Laramie, had waited for him. They never lost hope or gave up on each other. Johnny was discharged as a colonel and returned home. After rehabilitation and intense physical therapy, he and Dessa married and had a family. This disabled and highly decorated Marine became successful in business and went on to be involved in the development of a wheelchair basketball program for veterans. He was one of the truly great men in my life.

"I have to think the military wouldn't have wanted to see a ball player with my reputation shot up or killed. They kept me busy, but out of harm's way generally speaking.

"Whatever the case may have been, I was aboard a ship that could have been attacked by Japanese Zeroes or sunk by an enemy sub. I was grateful to God I was able to come out of the war unharmed.

"Our job was to pick up war casualties and get them to safety. My men and I believed we saved a lot of lives. Our crew delivered those boys to facilities where they could get medical care and rehabilitation. It wasn't a pleasant job to see all of that suffering. But it was our job. I had learned as a kid when you have a job to do, you do it. At different times we transported Army replacement troops to a variety of islands."

It was during this period that Kenny was promoted to captain.

There were times when some of the Marines went ashore and spent the nights sleeping in tents. At a stop in Guam, Kenny's group played a game of softball as they waited to return to their ship. Suddenly, a hand grenade was lobbed from the jungle at the new captain's feet.

Everybody froze. Without missing a beat, the former ball handler scooped the small explosive up and tossed it back into the undergrowth.

Kenny responded, "Nothing happened."

"Later, when a Navy security detail was sent out to search for the ordinance, an unexploded hand grenade was located. It was a dud."

He continued, "There were times on beaches when I had to lead my unit to hunt down a few enemy soldiers who were concealed. When they were hidden in caves we had to use smoke, to force them out for air and capture them.

"I went around the world twice," Kenny reflected. "The first time, I was out for over a year."

On his second trip around the world, Kenny was homeward-bound aboard the *U.S.S. Callan* on one of its final voyages of the war.

"We were transporting B-29 pilots from Calcutta, India, westward via the Suez Canal and the Mediterranean Sea. The final destination was Norfolk, Virginia. The trip was completed without incident."

Once back on US soil, Captain Sailors fulfilled his last months of active duty at a Naval base in Farragut, Idaho, where he was honorably discharged. He returned home to his family and re-enrolled at the University of Wyoming to complete his last year of college basketball eligibility.

Chapter 22

BASKETBALL FAME TO NATIONAL ACCLAIM

World War II officially ended in September 1945. The former Wyoming championship team was reassembled with several returning servicemen during the fall quarter. Kenny rejoined the group in December, after his discharge from the Marines. He had missed the first five games of the season but was back on the roster.

Wyoming was a part of "The Big 7 Conference," which granted many returning veterans an extra year of eligibility. The men were registered as graduate students to be allowed to play college basketball. The graduate designation became a problem later in tournament play.

The group jelled like never before. The war had given them a completely different perspective on what was important. In the new year, Coach Shelton's schedule took the team on a tour of the East Coast. Fan favorites from previous visits, the Cowboys drew over 18,000 spectators to Madison Square Garden on January 3, 1946. The game was against a very good Long Island University (LIU) team, coached by Clair Bee, who eventually became a Hall of Famer. The Cowboys would defeat LIU 57-42.

In that game, *Life* magazine contract photographer Eric Schaal took a shot of his own. Kenny pulled up for a jumper at the top of the key. His teammates watched closely and waited for him to sink the ball or pass off to number 27, Milo Komenich. The big man was prepared to receive the ball from the captain and go in for a lay-up.

The famous picture captured Sailors at the top of his leap. Kenny seemed suspended two feet above the hardwood. The ball in his right hand, the guide hand positioned perfectly on the side, just before he dropped it away. The other players were in the usual flat-footed position, with both feet on the floor. The ground-breaking photo flew around basketball land and introduced millions to the amazing possibilities the novel "jump shot" had to offer.

Coach Ray Meyer of DePaul would estimate Kenny's jump was often as high as three feet. With that photo, a perfect moment was captured and changed the future of the game.

Sailors commented, "I didn't always take the jump shot. Whenever I could see a teammate in a position to take an open shot I would stop, jump, and dump a pass off to that guy. He could then drive in for the

Signature jump shot of Kenny Sailors. From the 1946 University of Wyoming yearbook. (Photo courtesy of the American Heritage Center, University of Wyoming.)

lay-up. My teammates knew what to watch for and we worked together to make the points."

Pressing forward the Cowboys went on to become the number-one-ranked college team in the nation. Sailors led the Pokes to a 22-4 record. The team was looking forward to pursuing another NCAA title.

"The NCAA, however, denied us the opportunity to compete for another national championship. It was determined that we had too many post-graduate students on the team.

"We were the number one team in the nation, but couldn't play in the NCAA tournament. It was a disappointment for sure. Coach Shelton was upset, of course."

Despite the controversy and perceived injustice, the coach continued to lead his team with character and dignity. Life would go on beyond basketball. After all, the previous war years had left indelible marks on the lives of the University of Wyoming Cowboys. Those veterans had learned critical lessons about what was most important in life.

Kenny was reminded of wisdom gained over time. Words from his mother: "It doesn't matter how many times you get knocked down. *You get up and keep going.*" And from Ev Shelton, "Don't complain. You don't want people calling you a crybaby."

After the season, being chosen for the West team in the College All-Star game in New York was a fitting end note for Kenny. He tied for high-scoring honors and was unanimously selected as a consensus college and AAU All-American. This was the third time he had received the honor. Other recognition included a three-time Skyline Conference all-league performer and a four-year UW letterman.

In March of 1946, Kenny was one of the Cowboys selected to play in the postseason AAU tournament, then considered the best basketball in the country. He teamed up to play with All-American Jim Pollard for the San Diego Dons. Kenny had a provision: He was to be excused for an all-star charity game in New York City on March 30. The Dons made it to the AAU finals and the title game was that very date. With Sailors gone, the Dons lost in the championship game.

Final accolades for Sailors in the 1945-46 season were All-Skyline Conference selection and winner of the Helms Foundation Award as best college player in the United States. Kenny did not receive his honors because of his jump shot or his scoring average of 7.8 points per game. His passing, dribbling, and floor leadership were the attributes that caused him to be elevated above other individuals on the nation's basketball courts.

Kenny was at the pinnacle of his basketball fame and drew crowds wherever he played. One publicity activity he was included in was a motorcade in Manhattan organized by *TRUE*, a national magazine. One of the All-American teams he had been selected for was being honored. Kenny was photographed with other college celebrities such as George Mikan, who went on to be a pioneer in professional basketball.

With college basketball behind him, Kenny had a decision: where to go and what to do in the future. If he chose professional basketball, he would lose his amateur status and be unable to try out for the United States Olympic team. But, he could keep his home in Wyoming and make more money.

Marilynne knew how to make the most of Kenny's money—their money. Years before, she learned how to "make money by saving money." Because of that, Boky and Corn Tassel had some cash money to buy a piece of property in Laramie.

"We figured we could build a house on that land," Kenny recalled. "A Swedish friend of ours was willing to teach us how to construct a log home. He did. We did. And by golly, we built a solid house with a good foundation, dove-tailed logs, Scandinavian-style corners, and a fine roof." (As of 2024, that house stands in fine shape in Laramie, Wyoming.)

Kenny mused, "I hate to say I was interested in the money, but I had to face my responsibilities. I wasn't crazy about the idea of living on the East Coast. At that time, pro teams were only in big cities. I always loved basketball and now I had the opportunity to make a living for my family. I was interested in seeing what professional basketball had to offer me."

Chapter 23

PRO BASKETBALL LEAGUES

The major American sports of baseball, hockey, and football were joined by basketball when the Basketball Association of America (BAA) was formed in 1946. It was a time of instability; the BAA had an East and West division. The name would change to the National Basketball Association (NBA) in 1949.

Cities with BAA teams were Washington, Philadelphia, New York, Providence, Toronto, Boston, Chicago, St. Louis, Cleveland, Detroit, and Pittsburgh. Franchises folded and switched cities, which led to volatility and uphcaval.

The National Basketball League (NBL) was founded in 1937 and clustered in smaller cities. Businesses such as General Electric, Firestone, Goodyear, and others supported the teams. Members of the teams were then eligible for jobs in the company when they retired from the sport. The NBL and the BAA merged to form the NBA in 1949-50.

"I could have had a career in the Marines," Kenny said. "But I wanted to go home and continue to play more basketball. I went to Cleveland in 1946 and signed with the Rebels because they offered me the most money, $7,000 for the season. Can you imagine that? I believe the good Lord was watching out for us." Sailors was the highest-paid point guard in the league at that time.

He concluded, "I wanted to make enough money to take care of my family and be able to set aside a nest egg to establish a business when I was done with pro ball."

Dutch Dehnert was his coach with the Rebels. Kenny said, "Dehnert didn't like the idea that I didn't keep both feet on the ground and use a two-handed set shot. The coach said to me, 'Sailors, where'd yuse get that leapin' one-hander?' I said, Well, I've been using it a long time."

"Then he benched me."

"I decided to talk to the general manager. I told him I probably wasn't a good fit for the coaching style of the team and asked for a trade."

Kenny learned there were other wheels in motion. "Dehnert was on his way out and Roy Clifford came in. The new coach had no issue with me using my jump shot. I started and went on to average nearly 10 points a game as a rookie."

For income during the off-season, Kenny, Marilynne, and Cora had purchased a convalescent home for older women in Cheyenne in the summer of 1946. Marilynne and their daughter Linda lived with Cora, while Kenny made do in the cities he played in. Both women enjoyed working with the older ladies. Together, Marilynne and her mother-in-law made a good business team. The family kept the convalescent home until 1953, when they sold it to Kenny's sister and her husband, Gladys and Archie Smith.

Cleveland club owners informed Kenny in the summer of 1947 that the team was being dissolved. Sailors ended up with the Chicago Stags through the dispersal draft.

"They had absolutely *no need* for me," Kenny recalled. "The Chicago Stags sold me to the Philadelphia Warriors, who didn't need me either. I was finally sold to the Providence, Rhode Island Steamrollers and finished out the 1947-48 season with them."

Kenny said, "Providence was the only team that really used me. My son Dan was born in 1947, and I headed home to be with my family for a time before I returned to finish the year out. Mother continued to handle the convalescent home. Marilynne and I accepted an offer to manage the old Jackson Lake Lodge in Jackson Hole, Wyoming, that summer. On our days off, my wife and I planned to scout around northwest Wyoming for property to establish a Dude Ranch business. We found a place to buy in the area."

The Steamrollers were still in business at the beginning of the 1947-48 basketball season. Kenny was given regular playing time, which allowed him to become a leading scorer and playmaker for the team. Kenny especially enjoyed a fresh assignment from the management. Sailors held clinics to teach students about basketball, a relatively new sport. The ball handler enjoyed working with the younger kids. Later in life he would continue the basketball workshops and teach both boys and girls in rural Alaska.

While Kenny was in Providence, coaches seemed to come and go through a revolving door. The team did poorly and finished 6-42 with a shortened playing season.

"I was disgusted with all of the losses. But I was in it for the money. As long as I was getting paid I kept doing my job. They didn't miss sending me a paycheck, so I stayed."

The Steamrollers had an interesting surprise for Kenny. A genial man named George Nostrand bounced onto the team roster.

Kenny chuckled, "Now George was a good fella and I liked him. We had played college ball together at the University of Wyoming. He was tall, skinny, not too strong, and played inside. He just loped along down the floor and we nicknamed him Big George.

"There was this one game where I saw George parked under the basket. I jumped up to pass him the ball so he could go in for the lay-up. As I went into the air, George turned his back to me. Already in motion, I fired the ball. What do you know? My shot hit him in the back of the head, ricocheted off, bounced around the rim, and dropped through the cords! Big George turned around, rubbed his 'noggin,' and tried to figure out what in the world was going on. That was the craziest shot I ever made.

"To continue the goofiness, the officials could not figure out who to give the points to. Finally, it was determined that he would get the points because Big George had the last contact with the ball. I was given the assist on the bucket. A stunned radio announcer hooted, 'That has to be the greatest shot in basketball.'"

In the off-season of 1948, Kenny and Marilynne began to build their Dude Ranch business in northwest Wyoming and work with troubled boys.

During the second season with Providence in 1948-49, the Sailors family moved to the east coast. An unexpected medical crisis arose when Marilynne's emphysema and asthma became critical. An SOS was sent to Annie Hershiser, her aunt in Casper, Wyoming. Marilynne had lived with this dear woman during high school. Annie did not hesitate to hightail it to Rhode Island and help them in their desperate need.

Kenny related, "Annie was a grand old lady in her 70s. She spent the winter with us and cared for all of us. Without Annie's help, we would have had to return home to Wyoming. Boky and I thanked God for her."

Their son Dan remembered his mother's aunt years later, "My sister and I called her Aunt Hirschentoot." Leave it to those dear kids to inject some humor in a rough situation.

Kenny was named to the "All Pro" team, even though the Steamrollers had an 18-90 record for those years. At the end of that season, the Providence Steamrollers were no more, and the Sailors family moved back to Wyoming.

The Dude Ranch was beginning to take off in the summer of 1949. Kenny was able to build their clientele using marketing skills he had learned by observing promoters who were involved with professional

Playing for the original Denver Nuggets 1950. (Photo courtesy of Courtesy of the American Heritage Center University of Wyoming.)

basketball. He and Marilynne decided to add hunting and guiding to the fall calendar after the dudes had departed.

On July 16, 1949, Kenny signed as a free agent for that season with the original Denver Nuggets franchise in Colorado. He averaged 17.3 points and 4.0 assists per game. Many considered him the best ball-handler in the league. Kenny smiled as he recalled those days. "One thing I liked to do with a defender, was to get to rocking back and forth with him. Then surprise, he'd rock and I'd jump up and shoot.

"I was sure glad to be closer to home. My family came to games and we were able to spend much more time together."

It was not a pretty season for the Nuggets. Even though Sailors had a notable year in Denver, the team finished 11-51. At the bottom of the Western Division, they too, folded.

The Dude Ranch, now called the Heart Six, was a going enterprise during the summer of 1950. Plans were being made to discontinue the dudes and go strictly to hunting and guiding.

Wanting to finish his final year in league play, Sailors was sold by Denver to the Boston Celtics on June 22, 1950, for the 1950-51 season. He traveled to Boston while his family stayed in Laramie. All too soon, Kenny had another realization. "Here I was again, playing for a team that didn't need me. Bob Cousy was the starting guard and had a great reputation in Boston. The only way I kept going, was to be a high scorer and make plenty of assists."

While with the Celtics, Kenny roomed with Chuck Cooper, the first black player who played in an NBA game. Kenny liked Chuck and vice versa. "We had good conversations about race relationships and opportunities for blacks. The whole color thing didn't matter one bit to me. He and I became good friends."

Chuck told me, "It'll work out for blacks to play in the pros. It's just going to take a while."

Indeed.

Kenny could see the handwriting on the wall for him playing in Boston. He was nearly thirty years old and wanted to finish his career and settle down permanently in Wyoming with his family. Walter Brown, the owner of the Celtics, finally obliged the under-used point guard and traded him to the Baltimore Bullets on December 1, 1950. After ten games with the Celtics, it was down the coast to Maryland for Sailors.

While in "The Crab Cake Capital of the World," Kenny played in fifty games and averaged 9.5 points and nearly 3 assists per game. Sailors liked Baltimore.

In addition to his salary, Kenny had a surprise deal with the *Bennett Prune Juice* company. "The club didn't even ask me to be a spokesman. They just used my name and picture for advertising and received the money. Whatever that amount was. The Bennett company sent me plenty of their special elixir to keep my system regulated. It tasted okay but sure was different from the energy drinks of today. Of course I drank it. There was no way I'd let the stuff go to waste."

Kenny promotes prune juice while playing for the Baltimore Bullets. (Photo courtesy of Sailors family.)

Sailors was pleased he had Marilynne and the kids with him. For too many years Marilynne's respiratory issues had kept the family split up.

The Bullets management required Kenny to put on basketball clinics for Baltimore area high school students, to introduce them to the sport. Kenny enjoyed doing the clinics.

However, it was another losing season for Sailors with the Bullets.

"On the flip side of the coin," recalled Kenny, "I was playing with Belus Smawley, a man from North Carolina, who had developed a sort of twisting, fall-away jump shot."

The two hoopsters became good friends and even lived on the same street. Belus also ended up endorsing *Bennet's Prune Juice* as well. The two men and their wives often played cards together on free evenings.

When the season ended in 1951, Kenny had five years of pro basketball and was ready to quit pro sports. Ironically, he did not achieve NBA notoriety because he had the misfortune of being on teams that folded, not because he wasn't a great player.

Sailors played in the BAA for three years and then the NBA for two years.

Kenny had been away from home for two and a half years during the war and five years throughout his basketball career. He was missing a more stable family life and wanted to be home with his wife and children in Wyoming. He was ready to wrap up his basketball career. Sailors retired after the 1951 season. Cora would continue with the convalescent home in Cheyenne. Kenny and Marilynne would look forward to building their business in northwestern Wyoming.

Chapter 24

AFTER PRO BASKETBALL

Once the decision was made to retire from professional basketball, Kenny was offered college jobs as an assistant coach. Ev Shelton wanted him to coach the freshman team at Wyoming. Kenny hated to disappoint the best coach he'd ever had but didn't want to coach.

He said, "I had zero interest in coaching. I rejected all offers I received from college and high schools. The Lord began to show me there were more important things in life than sports. I knew I needed to move in another direction."

The off-season of professional basketball for Kenny allowed for several business opportunities. "We considered making arrangements with my mother for her to take charge of the Convalescent Home and we could look for an opportunity to move out of town."

"Marilynne's breathing problems weighed heavy on our hearts. Over the years we had visited various doctors in the cities where I had played. She was given the typical prescriptions for steroids and inhalers. I was shocked when one physician stated that Marilynne will be lucky to live until she is 50."

Stunned, I asked, "What can we do differently?"

The doctor offered this advice. "Move out of the city, away from the congestion with all the hustle and bustle. Trade in the fast pace of life for somewhere in the country where activities are less frantic and stressful. Go someplace where you step into another lifestyle."

Another lifestyle. Wasn't that the million-dollar question?

.....

After a game when the Cleveland Rebels had played with the Washington Capitals in 1947, former Wyoming governor, Nels Smith, approached Kenny with a business deal. Nelson Rockefeller, who owned the old Jackson Lake Lodge, was looking for a young couple to manage his facility. Rockefeller had heard of Kenny Sailors and liked what he knew of the cager. He wondered if the couple would come to work at the lodge.

Kenny reflected, "The years I played college and pro basketball had interfered with my hunting. This looked like an opportunity to return to a way of life my wife and I missed."

"I was surprised when this offer came out of the blue. I said I was interested but needed to talk to my wife. When I did, Marilynne thought it was a good chance to move to a place we both wanted to live. We said yes to the offer."

Even though they'd spent their lives in Wyoming, neither Kenny nor Marilynne had ever been to Jackson Hole before.

"The first sight of the Grand Tetons was breathtaking," Kenny remembered. "We knew this was a place we could fit into very easily. When we had time off from working at the lodge, we drove around the area and noticed there were dude ranches for sale. It didn't take us long to start looking for a place of our own.

"When we arrived at the Jackson Lake Lodge, we learned it was one of the largest and most active establishments in the area. It was a beautiful structure with eight guest rooms on the second floor of the main building. Numerous large pictures and original paintings of the stunning area scenery filled the soaring spaces. Downstairs were two large rooms. One was for dancing and entertainment, and the other a spacious dining room. Outside the main building, there were forty rustic cabins. Believe me, they were rustic. Each building had a double bed and a cookstove for warmth and to prepare food, if desired. Behind each cabin was a personal outhouse for the necessary business. Some of the guests were surprised by that inconvenience. Our family lived in a cabin close to the main lodge."

The Rockefellers did not hire locally. Help was brought in from the East Coast as chefs, wait staff, housekeepers, maintenance crews, entertainers, and business employees.

"My wife managed the kitchen and dining room, which could seat 200 guests. We could use a pickup from the Lodge and drive into Idaho Falls to grocery shop. Marilynne ordered the food, saw to meal schedules, and dealt with the public. State regulations would not allow any wild game to be prepared and served.

"I managed the help, which meant I was in charge of dealing with personnel problems. I settled squabbles over stolen tips or silly stuff when people sniped at each other. Many folks were good workers with a nice attitude. Others just seemed to be on the peck.

"I had to explain basic wildlife habits to city dwellers. I chased porcupines from under cabins, which ladies thought *must* have been grizzly bears. I kept repairmen on the job with maintenance tasks they weren't always familiar with or didn't know how to use the tools. I set up recreational activitiesm which included dances, picnics, fishing, and climbing mountains. I was able to start float trips on the river and begin picnics and camping trips up north to Yellowstone Park.

"We learned so much and enjoyed many aspects of the job," Kenny recalled. "We loved the area and the pay was good. The dances we had scheduled were well attended by the guests. Many locals came to enjoy the evening events on the weekend as well. Folks of all ages especially enjoyed Western music and activities.

"What we did not like," Kenny stated, "was the language and jokes the masters of ceremonies thought they had to throw in. The entertainers became a problem for us. I figured because families and children were participating, there should be decent standards set. I talked with the Rockefellers and requested a change in that regard. The MCs changed but the inappropriate language did not. Marilynne and I were disturbed by the lack of common sense and decency. We talked to the owners and informed them we planned to resign at the end of the season."

Kenny went on, "My family and I continued to tour around the area when we had free time. We heard about a ranch in a beautiful setting with great views of the Teton Mountains. The 'Boggy Bench' was owned by an old fella named Dad Turner and his wife. They were interested in selling and we were interested in taking a look at what they had. We fell in love with the place right away and figured we might as well see if we could make a deal.

"The Turners talked. We talked. The four of us talked. We agreed on a purchase price of $45,000. We had money for a down payment and would be required to make two payments per year until the balance was paid. Included in the package were fifty acres of deeded land with thirty-five acres of that along the river. There was a modern main lodge with electricity and running water plus an additional eight rustic cabins, a barn, sheds, and outbuildings. A Forest Service lease option for 2,300 acres was a part of the deal and would be used for our horse pasture as well as guest trail rides.

"Lucky for us," remarked Kenny, "Marilynne had tucked away more of my basketball pay than I had realized. I appreciated how well she had handled our funds.

"We decided this would be a great place for us to live and start a dude ranch and guiding business. The spot would be perfect for Marilynne because of her breathing issues. Fresh air and getting away from city life was just what the doctor ordered."

The couple finished their first and last season as managers of the Jackson Lake Lodge in September of 1947.

Sixty-five years later, Kenny would notice where their former Heart Six Ranch had sold for $13 million.

Chapter 25

HEART SIX RANCH

Kenny had carefully planned for his future beyond basketball.

"I decided during the basketball off-season that I wanted to get into the dude ranching and guiding business. I had played for too many teams that had gone under. I knew I could fall back on my hunting if I needed to make a living."

In the spring of 1948, the Sailors family traveled forty miles north-east of Jackson Hole, to their new place near Moran, Wyoming. On the advice of Dad Turner, the previous owner, Kenny had retained Turner's former employee, Dutch Olson. An old cowboy and seasoned veteran of Wyoming winters, Olson was familiar with the guiding business. Sailors figured it would be wise to keep that fella on the payroll. "Dutch stayed at the ranch during the winter and took care of the horses. I learned a lot from him.

"The Turners had called the ranch Dad's Place. An earlier nickname was Boggy Bench. I decided to buy an old, registered Wyoming cattle brand that had belonged to my aunt Hattie at the Brooklyn Lodge. We named our place the Heart Six Ranch after the brand. We loved our new home and the magnificent views of the Grand Tetons."

Marilynne and horses with a backdrop of the Grand Teton Mountains. (Photo courtesy of Sailors family.)

"We were ready to get to work," Kenny stated. "Before long we built a larger barn with more stalls and hay storage. We improved the water system by developing the natural spring. Water lines were added to the buildings and new cabins were constructed. The water improvements were especially appreciated.

"Other amenities we added were a volleyball court, basketball hoop, space for other games, chairs, and benches along a fire pit. We had a few head of cattle and of course, plenty of horses. There was lots of space for kids—Sailors' kids, or camper kids. The youngsters could enjoy being kids in the high country of the Cowboy State."

Dan said, "My sister Linda and I loved growing up on the Heart Six. She and I had our room in a big open area upstairs in the main lodge. Big windows in our room gave us a great view of the ranch. From that special observation post, we kept track of everything from wildlife and weather to who was coming up the road. Not much escaped our keen eyes.

"The barns, sheds, and corrals were a never-ending source of entertainment. Believe me. We made the most of them. When the boys and dudes were around in the summer, we were constantly in motion. Over the years we met some interesting young guys. One of them was a fella named Dave Lowe, who was from Boston.

"Of course, Pop made sure we learned responsibility by helping with chores. One winter chore for Linda and me was hauling water in a barrel, on a sled from the river. The water always slopped around

Kenny, Dan, Cora, Linda and Marilynne in the early 1950's.
(Photo courtesy of Sailors family.)

and froze on the two of us. That was not fun. Like any other job, it had to be done and we just learned to do it.

"Another job for Linda was to help Mom in the kitchen. Even though we had cooks through the years, my sister became a good cook and a pretty decent pie baker."

Education was another important issue for the family.

According to Kenny, "Our ranch in the Moran community was sort of close to a one-room country schoolhouse. Linda and Dan both acquired their grade school education in that log building.

"The school had a wood stove in a corner of the room. "The cloakroom was in the back of the building and had one wall lined with coat hooks. Near the door, a wooden stand supported a two-gallon pottery water jar with a metal spigot at the bottom, to release water for drinking. Around the side of the building was a pumpjack for drawing water from a well.

"The students took turns performing daily jobs for the teacher. The water bucket would be filled at the pump. A slop bucket in front of the water jar had to be dumped. Blackboards needed to be erased and the erasers cleaned by slapping them against the steps or the fence. Floors were swept with a corn straw broom. During the winter months, paths needed to be shoveled around the schoolyard and to the front gate.

"Of course, the outhouses behind the school, one for boys and one for girls, also needed to be swept with the broom. Any cobwebs in the corners of the little building were knocked down using the broom. The last chore was replenishing old catalogs. They were used as toilet paper and set on the seats of the buildings out back."

"To get to school," Dan remembered, "We usually walked the three miles. If it was snowy, we might get a ride. But generally, we traveled by 'shanks ponies.'"

Kenny smiled, "Boky decided she would like to be involved in the education process. She was chairman of the school board for a time and did a good job. Marilynne had studied education in college.

"When the kids were old enough to attend high school, they rode a school bus around thirty-five miles, into Jackson Hole. Both of the kids graduated from twelfth grade at that school."

Dan commented, "When I was young, I had no idea my dad had been involved in pro basketball. It was quite a few years before I knew what Kenny Sailors was famous for.

"Some folks thought maybe I'd be a chip off the old block in that department and get into basketball. I wasn't too interested in being inside on a hardwood court. Instead, I headed for the forest and went into downhill skiing. I ended up with a spectacular flying crash on the slopes and broke my leg. That took care of my sports career.

"Later on, I started flying in another way.

"I became good friends with the guy from Boston who had come to our guest ranch. This kid was older than me and had a grandmother who had quite a bit of money. Dave knew about airplanes and flew to the Heart Six. Birds and animals always interested my dad, and I picked up on that. I'd even wondered about being in the sky. Now I had a chance to find out what that would be like. I was bitten by the flying bug.

"Dave Lowe took me under his wing, so to speak, and began to teach me about flying. We'd bump down a grass runway away from the ranch buildings. My mom would watch us through her binoculars trying not to fret. We always came back in three pieces: the plane, Dave, and me. I was hooked. I kept flying."

The idea for a boy's ranch had sprouted in Kenny's mind after he returned from WWII.

"I had a wonderful Christian mother who raised my brother and me well. But I knew what I had missed in not having a father. I looked for ways to be a positive male influence for fatherless boys.

"We could run the boy's ranch program in the summer months, then in the fall, we would switch to hunting and guiding. In the off-season, I had time for civic and community activities."

The Sailors figured out a marketing plan.

“My guiding business and basketball career provided me with good contacts in other states. I traveled around the country to share my ideas with families who might be interested in such an outdoor program for their boys. I guess I’d picked up a few ideas from promoter Ned Irish when I played basketball at Madison Square Garden, in New York City.

“The first year during the winter at the Heart Six, I traveled the country, showing movies and describing the wholesome opportunities we had available. I talked with parents and teachers, promoting the idea that we had a good place to send boys for the summer. Horseback riding was an activity that caught the attention of many audiences.

“Each five-week program was designed to accommodate boys ages nine to fifteen. Every kid had a horse and learned to care for his cayuse. That included feeding and grooming the horse and taking responsibility for their horse tack.

“I always went along on pack trips. The boys came from all over the country: New York to California, Minnesota to Texas. To say we had an interesting mix was an understatement. I usually had a couple of cowboys along on trips to help supervise and teach the ‘greenhorns’ how to handle their ponies.

“We thought it was important to have professional counselors or teachers on staff. Some of the boys came from troubled situations where their parents were split up. I assumed professionals such as those we hired would have been familiar with being in charge of kids. I was barking up the wrong tree. Many of those adults worked well in a structured setting, but were not equipped to function independently, in the out of doors.”

Chapter 26

DUDE RANCH

"In some ways," Kenny said, "setting up the boys' program was a bit like setting up a new basketball team. Some participants came highly recommended. However, you didn't know what you had until you put them through the paces and could see what they were made of.

"Most all of the boys and the hired help we had were new to the type of experience we offered at the Heart Six. The learning curve was steep for all of the participants. Taking care of the horses was one thing. Getting a cayuse saddled, a rider onto the horse and *then* riding, was quite another.

"The boys did pretty well with those assignments. The adults had a few more problems. There was this one psychologist we hired, who had a doctorate. Try as we might, we could never help that guy figure out how to saddle his horse. In five weeks, it never happened.

"Sometimes there are just some things that don't seem to come together in a new environment. We finally worked out a plan for another staff person to partner with that fella to get him safely saddled up. What a deal that was.

"Those boys just ate the whole thing up. We'd ride into the mountains of the Teton Wilderness area and wander through some of the prettiest country you'd ever want to see. The youngsters practiced roping and then would move on to fishing, hiking, climbing mountains, or playing in the snow. They even swam in the mountain lakes, which were not warm by any stretch of the imagination.

"If those city mothers could have seen their little darlings, after ten days in the wilderness, they might have flipped their wigs. It was a dream come true for boys in that era, where cowboys like Roy Rogers were the king of the hill. They loved riding those cayuses in the wild. Not having to take a bath and make their beds was like icing on the cake.

"We also allowed our participants to train with firearms through an affiliation with the National Rifle Association (NRA). There was plenty of space on the ranch which allowed us to have a fifty-foot rifle range set up away from the buildings, where it could be safely monitored. The boys used .22 rifles under close supervision. Important rules on responsible handling of firearms and decision-making were taught. Anyone not obeying these rules lost their privileges. Period."

The program went pretty well for a spell. Kenny and Marilynne had set a high bar. They chose to hire responsible counselors and cowboys to work with their boys. As time went on, it became a challenge to hire individuals who had good common sense and operated responsibly in the wild.

An incident occurred that brought the boys' program to a halt.

"I always went on the pack trips and took responsibility for the activity," said Kenny. "I had cowboys along, but they never did supervise the kids."

An early summer pack trip was planned for a campout high in the mountains at Crater Lake. "Once we arrived at our site," Kenny recalled, "we observed open water in the middle of the lake. The ice extended out some distance from the bank to the edge of the water. I made a point to inform everyone about the dangers of the situation.

"We had begun setting up camp when one of the cowboys from the ranch rode in. He informed me an important matter had to be resolved and I was needed back at the Heart Six.

"I was between a rock and a hard spot. In the early 1950s, the only way to communicate in the mountains was person to person.

"I didn't have a choice in the matter. I would have to return to the Heart Six. The ride to the ranch would take me a day, as would the return trip. Before leaving, I talked with the counselors and cowboys, reminding them to keep safety first and keep a sharp eye on the boys.

"When I left those adults in charge, I emphasized I'd return as soon as possible. I figured they should know the ropes by then.

"What was I thinking?

"When I returned from the Heart Six and came into view of the lake, I was horrified at what I saw! Hoof prints were decorating the edges of that icy lake.

"The folks I left in charge had let the kids go out on that rotten ice. They let them ride out on the ice with their horses. I about flipped my wig!

"When I asked what was going on, the adults sheepishly confessed."

"We didn't see any reason the kids couldn't try something a little different, as long as they stayed close to the bank and away from the open water."

What were they thinking? They weren't.

"When the dust settled and we got back to the ranch, I had a heart-to-heart talk with my wife." I said, "Boky, this is it. We're done. I can just see somebody getting killed and me getting blamed for it. We're done. Period!

"I did not leave anyone else in charge of my camps after that. We finished the season out and that was the end of the boys' program. From then on we only did guided hunting trips."

Chapter 27

BE WHAT IT TAKES

"I've been in excellent shape my whole life," Kenny noted. "Growing up as I did on a farm, the entire family was active. We had no choice. As my mother had reminded me, 'If you don't work, you don't eat.' Certainly, I wanted to eat. Plus, the work we did kept us in top shape whether we liked it or not. Mother always made sure we ate well with basic, healthy foods. I guess I just got used to it and developed a good habit of taking care of myself. Later on, my wife Marilynne adopted the same type of philosophy.

"Another thing, playing basketball required being in good shape. We ran, ran, ran, for Coach Shelton. As a Marine, conditioning and PT (physical training) were a big deal for being combat ready.

"I didn't think about it at the time, but the Marine Corps helped me toward becoming a big game hunting guide in another way. I was taught how to use a 30.06 rifle. That's the first big gun I ever fired. We trained on that firearm and also learned how to handle a pistol. All the officers carried 45s as a personal weapon. Later, the 30.06 was a popular hunting rifle, often used by veterans.

"There was certainly a common thread that ran through my life. I was always around horses. I loved the outdoors and learned to hunt early. I acquired additional firearms training in the military. I wouldn't say these things were easy, but each one became a strong component in my life and business. I was thankful to the Good Lord for everything.

"Learning to be in control of my emotions was important also. Control helped me make good shots with my rifle as a kid, as a Marine, and as an outfitter. Successful basketball scoring came through control. Practice-practice-practice and the will to persevere pulled everything together to get the job done, no matter what my assignment was.

"My mother found plenty of ways to keep me humble and keep my emotions in check. I found that when I took time to recognize others, listen to folks, and give them a chance to shine, good relationships were built. She was quite a woman, my mother.

"No matter what you do in life, you've got to hustle when you're first starting. Be sincere and put your best foot forward. Whether you're trying to make a favorable impression on a new basketball coach, starting a job, or guiding hunters, do your best. Until the coach, the boss, or hunters know what you can do, you're just one of many.

"Believe in yourself. The person who is in charge must become familiar with your skills and believe in you. You've got to earn people's respect. Do the right thing and you'll go far. Lastly, stay close to the Good Lord, He will help bring the details together.

"There were similarities between shooting a basketball and shooting a gun. Each activity requires patience and dedication to learn. There is no payoff unless you are accurate. You miss the basket, and you miss the animal when hunting."

Kenny Sailors had grown up without a father to come alongside him at important times in life. His mother made it a point to stand on what she had been taught by the words of Scripture.

Her father had imparted principles of faith, discipline, and character, which allowed her to persevere in the catastrophes of life. Rather than be derailed, Cora moved forward as an overcomer. She did not give up. She believed she would raise boys to become men. Men who would make a difference.

.....

Back to those days in the dirt in front of the windmill at Hillsdale, Kenny had faced his problem head-on by saying, "Why not me? I can jump."

Instead of retreating to whine, "Why is Bud such a meanie? I'll never make a shot in that hoop." He did not give up, but he kept looking up. As he looked up, he was inspired.

Kenny did not succeed in everything. He sure was not perfect. However, he was willing to try something different and see what could result. He looked for the good even when he experienced setbacks, disappointments, heartbreak, and personal calamities. It was in those moments that the words of Cora Houtz Sailors would ring in his spirit: "It doesn't matter if you get knocked down seven times. *You get back up!*"

Erin, a family member, said of Kenny, "He was one of the nicest men ever and made me a better person because of who he was. I always knew he would take time to listen and encourage.

I knew I could depend on him when I needed a hand up. He would be there to give it."

Chapter 28

WYOMING GUIDING

"Guiding at the Heart Six was always interesting," Kenny said. "But the hunts that stick in your mind are the ones where something strange happens."

"Take the case of the client with impaired vision.

"I had guided a client onto a hillside and got him set up to wait for the deer to come through the meadow below him. I moved up to the hill through the timber to scout for the game. Suddenly, I heard a bang. And then I heard a second shot. I thought, is a bear attacking?

"I was positioned above my sight-impaired hunter and figured I'd be safer if I kept the trees between us. He was standing with his gun, firing in every direction.

"I hollered as I walked into the clearing."

Pointing all over he exclaimed, "I know I got one here, here, and over there."

"He had seen deer come by and shot at anything that moved. By then, it was too dark to scout the area. We saddled up and headed back to the lodge.

"The next morning, we returned to the scene of the shoot-out. We found no evidence of animals, dead or alive. This man had planned throughout his life to come on a Wyoming hunt. The only thing he shot was his shadow.

"That experience was a wake-up call for me to realize all clients were not seasoned hunters. Safety first became our highest priority."

"Another unusual hunt involved three fellows. Two came from Chicago with a friend. These men had saved money for their dream hunt. The friend was not only inexperienced but in poor physical shape. The size of the man was a problem for the horse. Riding the horse was a problem for the man. He ended up saddle sore and stiff. The next day, both were hurting. They stayed in camp.

"The following day one of the other men returned to camp with an elk. Now the big guy was ready to hunt, even though he was saddle sore. I walked him through a meadow where we had staked the horses. Mule deer had been sighted nearby, and the man sat down to watch and wait.

"I hiked uphill to move the game into the meadow. I heard one shot, which I thought was strange. I returned to the hunter."

He glanced up. "I shot one."

"I walked to where he pointed. Wouldn't you know it? He had shot and wounded one of my horses. All we could do was put it down. The worst part was this horse belonged to my daughter Linda.

"The old boy felt so bad. He offered to pay for the horse. While I didn't like having my horse shot, I recognized it was an accident. The man wouldn't be consoled. Soon the other guys had enough and just wanted to get out. We packed up and headed for the homestead.

"We did everything possible to give our clients a memorable experience. But when things go haywire, you have to cut your losses and move forward. From then on we implemented practices which would keep people and the horses separated."

Kenny had upbeat stories to share as well. "Vance Burch, a sixteen-year-old, came for a three-day hunt in September of 1959 with Bob Bump a family friend."

Vance told his story. “We stayed in a very rustic cabin with cracks in the wooden floors and the log walls. The only light was a bulb, dangling from the ceiling, with a pull chain on one side. A pot-bellied stove stood in the middle of the room with two beds crowded in.”

“On the first night, Bob woke me up. ‘Vance, are you cold’”?

“I was freezing. Bob got up and stoked the fire.”

“The next night Bob woke me up again. ‘Vance, do you hear anything’”?

“What’s that wailing and yipping,” I asked.

“Just some old coyotes singing to each other,” Bob chuckled. “Let’s let them sing us back to sleep.”

“Mornings were chilly. We moved fast to reach the lodge, warm up, and eat breakfast.

“I wore a special bone-handled knife on my belt my father had brought me from Vienna, Austria. Kenny made me feel important when he asked to see it and exclaimed over it.

“I didn’t bag an elk that trip. But I never forgot the coyotes, the Heart Six, and Kenny Sailors.”

……

Kenny was a natural storyteller. One story was a personal Wyoming moose tale.

“One winter afternoon, Boky noticed a moose wandering up the plowed road to our lodge.”

She called out, “Kenny the cook is coming soon. Get that moose out of the yard so he won’t attack anybody.”

“With a whoop and holler, I started throwing snowballs at the critter. The darn thing wouldn’t move. I grabbed a coat to shoo him off. He didn’t even flick an ear. I figured I’d just dust him off with a little birdshot, which wouldn’t hurt him. I went into the house and loaded my .45.

"Outside, the moose was facing the opposite direction. I aimed and fired. The birdshot tapped his behind and made him mad. He swung around. Then he commenced to charge.

"When moose get agitated, they move fast and make a mess of whoever is in their way.

"I took off. Glad I could sprint. The bull was charging, kicking his front feet to slash me. My sweet wife had witnessed the whole incident and threw the door wide open for me.

"I was full steam ahead and dived over the threshold just as the moose lunged.

"I was saved! The big bull was stopped by the door frame, his horns too big for the opening.

"I'd never had such concentration. Not even in Madison Square Garden during the championship basketball game. That moose had my undivided attention. Period.

"To add insult to injury, Boky couldn't contain her laughter. 'I knew he couldn't get you Corn Tassel. He was too big for the door.'"

Chapter 29

PATRIOTISM

Kenny recalled, "My mother was very patriotic and civic-minded. When we lived on the farm she participated in community activities as often as she could. It was important for her to be informed and she never missed a chance to vote. She taught Bud and me how to apply Scriptural principles in our daily lives to become better citizens.

"My brother and I absorbed the example modeled by our mother. While Bud and I served during World War II, we formed very firm convictions of what America stood for and why we believed in our country."

As pro basketball wound up for Kenny in 1951, his family lived with Cora at the Convalescent Home in Cheyenne. The family had a second daughter, Carrie, who had been born to Kenny and Marilynne in the late 1940s. Injured at birth, she had Cerebral Palsy and required extra care. It is possible that she resided in a medical care facility.

"When I was younger," son Dan recalled, "I didn't remember my little sister. I did remember that my folks would leave Linda and me with Grandma, and tell us they were going to visit her."

In Cheyenne, Kenny worked as the recreation director for the city. He said, "I was busy working with the youth and overseeing sports programs in the community. Baseball, basketball, soccer, swimming, and tennis were all popular. The public facilities that we could use were limited. I juggled schedules that included small city gyms and the use of school and church buildings or fields. I also initiated a "Golden Ager" group, as I felt retired folks should have some opportunities for group activities as well."

Judge Frank A. Barrett, a friend, approached Kenny. "I think you are the type of person who would represent Laramie County well in the Wyoming State House of Representatives."

Kenny was flattered, but skeptical. "I don't know much about politics. I usually seem to be on the other side of current issues."

The Judge responded, "That's not uncommon. Are you willing to learn? You have a solid background and a good work ethic. As a basketball player, you have good name recognition around the county which can work to your advantage."

Barrett, a U.S. Senator, continued, "Kenny, you owe it to your state to be involved in the political process."

"I couldn't turn down the chance to be involved in helping my home state. I agreed to give the campaign a try."

Kenny won the 1954 election and served in the Wyoming Legislature for two sessions in 1955 and 1956.

But it wasn't easy.

"The whole political process was hard to understand. I realized early in my political career that a person couldn't be an idealist. You might have thoughts, but there were many legislators to be convinced on the merit of your ideas. Lawmakers won't always vote with you even if they think you're right, because they don't want to cross party lines. I recognized as a new legislator, it was important to study and understand why the Founding Fathers created America as a Democratic Republic. I was grateful for what I learned."

Senator Barrett also encouraged Kenny to become involved in the Wyoming Boy's State program in the 1940s. Junior boys throughout the state were selected from their schools for a week of political and legislative activity. Sailors relished his involvement with the yearly gathering and participated for nineteen years.

"I enjoyed the program tremendously," Kenny said. "I started out handling the morning flag and pledge activities. During the week-long gathering, I taught a morning class on government. In the afternoon we went into the Mock Legislature. I became the parliamentarian of that legislative assembly and taught the kids how to write and present bills. Students would go on to debate each bill and proceed through the voting process. Important concepts were explored, and future state leaders were being developed. The kids loved it.

"It was great to be able to share my experiences from the campaign trail with the young men at Boys State. With my participation in the legislative process, I could speak to the difference one person can make."

It was during this time that their youngest daughter Carrie died.

Kenny reflected, "That was a hard time for all of us. My wife and I didn't get emotional about things," he commented sadly. "I think it helped to have my mother with us. She understood what it was to lose a baby girl. In Mother's case, it was three baby girls who died in Nebraska."

In 1959, President Dwight D. Eisenhower invited Kenny Sailors to come to the White House and participate in a national security discussion on foreign policy concerning possible Soviet aggression. Sailors had gained recognition for his understanding of political issues and his common-sense approach to dealing with difficult situations. Other participants in the group included former President Harry Truman, former Truman Secretary of State Dean Atcheson, Wyoming Senator John C. O'Mahony, and John Foster Dulles, Secretary of State for President Eisenhower. Kenny appreciated being a part of such a prestigious group and added valuable insight to the gathering.

"My friends encouraged me to run for office again in 1960, this time for the US House of Representatives. I just didn't have a good understanding of the political machinery. I campaigned around the state and did my best, but the party leadership was backing other candidates and I lost."

Senator Barrett continued to believe Kenny's name recognition would move his career forward. Again, he encouraged Kenny to stay on the campaign trail in both the US House race of 1962 and the US Senate race of 1964. It was not to be. Kenny lost those two races as well. He had been the chairman of the Barry Goldwater campaign in Wyoming during the 1964 Presidential election. Goldwater also lost.

In the face of the losses, Kenny Sailors did not bad-mouth his opponents.

"When I lost the third election, that was the nudge we needed to move to Alaska."

Chapter 30

ALASKA

In early 1943 before they married, Kenny and Marilynne discussed a future life in Alaska. It seemed like the time had arrived for them to follow up on their dreams. By 1965, their daughter Linda was married and living in Idaho. Son, Dan, had completed high school and thought he would like to pursue the rodeo life. The couple could get serious and make plans to head to the "Last Frontier."

"Boky's breathing was a big consideration for us," Kenny commented. "Years ago, doctors had encouraged us to consider moving to a lower elevation—somewhere under 3,000 feet, due to her breathing difficulties. Certain areas of Alaska met that criteria.

"The wildness and scope of the state beckoned us. We knew there would be opportunities to set up another hunting and guiding operation outside of the continental United States."

For Kenny and Marilynne, it would be a matter of drawing on past experiences to start over. There had been times when they had tried and failed. But more often they tried until they succeeded. They'd faced both opportunities and obstacles in their life together. A college chance on a date and a dance. Marriage when parents did not support them. Marine regulations and restrictions. Sleeping on park benches in San Diego. Help from a Christian Palestinian family in California. Difficult separations during pro basketball. The loss of a sweet daughter. Work with spoiled boys. Disappointments in politics. They were committed to each other and moved forward toward new goals and experiences.

Once again, Kenny figured, "If guiding didn't work out I knew we could homestead and live off the land. After all, Boky was a crack shot. If I didn't bring home some meat, she could. We wouldn't starve.

"My brother Bud and his friend Jeff Stone, a Navy commander, offered to buy the Heart Six from us. We worked out a deal and sold it to them. Mother was pleased Bud would live in Wyoming, even though I was leaving."

Kenny and Marilynne had never been to Alaska (aka Seward's Icebox). They researched how they needed to get ready to drive the ALCAN (Alaska Canada Highway).

"With information from *The Milepost* magazine, we found important pointers for driving the highway between Dawson Creek, British Columbia, and Fairbanks, Alaska. The message came through loud and clear: This trip would not be quick or easy.

"We paid attention to all the information we could find. It was a long list: Be prepared for long stretches of lonely gravel roads. Watch out for semis, they kicked up debris. A rock could hit your windshield and break it completely out. Stop for moose. If you hit one, it will total your car. If you see a car at the side of the road, get out to see if help is needed. Be sure to have plenty of gas. Get your car checked over before leaving. Take spare tires.

"No joke! We're not in Kanas anymore."

Kenny continued, "It was a good thing we checked the requirements for driving the 1,400 miles of the ALCAN. We packed our four-wheel-drive pickup and Airstream trailer with must-haves for the trip. The authorities thoroughly checked the supplies we carried."

The time arrived. They hitched their wagon to a star and headed north.

Kenny noted, "Our border crossing from Canada into Alaska came on July 4, 1965. We stopped at the first store we found so I could buy a fishing license. I wanted to make my arrival official.

"I wasn't paying attention to the time of day. The summer solstice was upon us and the sky was still bright. We were close to where a friend of mine lived, so we figured we'd just drop in. We knocked on the door. When he opened up to us, he thought we were crazy! It was three-thirty in the morning under the midnight sun. We had a brief visit and left. They went back to bed.

"Dust was a problem with the gravel road. Marilynne was having trouble breathing as the particles gathered in her throat. At Glennallen, we headed south on the Richardson Highway to Valdez. Soon Boky was sick.

"She needed a doctor and medicine. The only hospital we knew of between Whitehorse and Anchorage was in Glennallen. The dust was killing her. We just couldn't get away from it."

Marilynne finally said, "Kenny, I can't go anymore."

He turned their rig around and headed back up the road to Glennallen. The couple had noticed a sign for McMahan's Trailer Park on the Tok Cutoff road and stopped to park their trailer and head west to Faith Hospital in Glennallen. They hoped to get medicine for Marilynne and return to their travel.

"Marilynne was hospitalized for several days. After her release, we headed south to Valdez. Once more, Marilynne choked up. This time we stopped in the town of Chitina. Then it was back to Glennallen."

Discouraged, but not daunted, the Sailors pointed the truck west towards Anchorage. This time, only ten miles passed before Marilynne said, "We've got to stop." The couple returned to Faith Hospital.

"It seemed like we needed to stay put so her breathing could get straightened out. The bottom line was, it seemed like the good Lord knew we needed to be right there. He had His hand on us."

The Sailors returned to the Gakona trailer court owned by the McMahan's. Kenny made a quick decision. "What the heck, let's just stay here. The place isn't fancy, but it has everything we need."

Once the trailer was set up, Kenny headed back the fourteen miles to Glennallen to check out job possibilities in the Copper River Valley.

Marilynne and Daphne McMahan finally had a chance to sit down to visit. It was to be the beginning of a long-standing friendship.

Daphne talked about her family. "My husband Cleo has a guiding and hunting business. We have an older daughter plus a daughter and two boys who are still in high school and like sports."

Marilynne told her, "My husband Kenny was a guide and outfitter in Wyoming. He also played basketball for the Boston Celtics in the NBA." When she heard the word basketball, Daphne sat up a little straighter in her chair.

Meanwhile, back in Glennallen, Kenny was poking around town. He learned a new US Post Office was being built and more construction help was needed. He followed the lead and landed a job on the project for that summer.

When Kenny returned to the trailer court, the former Wyomingites sat down for a serious conversation. They needed to discuss the opportunities which had risen up before them, in the land of the midnight sun.

Chapter 31

GLENNALLEN SCHOOL OPPORTUNITIES

Daphne McMahan was involved in the community and on the Glennallen school board. She often discussed thoughts and issues with her husband.

"There's a new couple who just set up in the trailer court," Daphne informed Cleo. "The name is Sailors. Marilynne has some health issues and her husband Kenny is a guide and outfitter. Now imagine this? He played for the Boston Celtics and has an education degree.

"I'm heading into town. I'll visit with the superintendent and see if we might find a volunteer coach and maybe hire a teacher."

Daphne drove to the school and soon shared her information on Kenny Sailors, the new guy in the area. In no time, the superintendent was making haste up the road to the Gakona trailer court to meet with Mr. Sailors.

After introducing himself, the school administrator laid out the needs of the district. "We can't pay you much because we don't have any money. We're in a huge state with a small tax base. That's why we're short on staff. As a result, we don't have girls' sports."

Kenny paused. "I'd like the girls in this area to have sports opportunities. My daughter Linda was a good athlete and benefited from those programs. I don't even know if I'm going to stay in Glennallen. However, if I do, I'll consider giving you a hand any way I can to coach the girls here. I don't need to be paid."

The Superintendent added, "Mr. Sailors, would there by chance be any classes could you teach?"

Kenny looked at the possible employer. "Well, I have a background in government, history, social studies, and physical education."

Mr. Superintendent looked at the potential teacher. "Well, Mr. Sailors, I believe we just might be able to make a deal."

A deal, indeed. A signed teaching contract and a volunteer coach for the school year. The Superintendent was happy, as were Kenny and Marilynne. The Chechakos, or new Alaskans, were set for a new adventure in life. Kenny remarked, "There was no way I thought I'd get back into basketball."

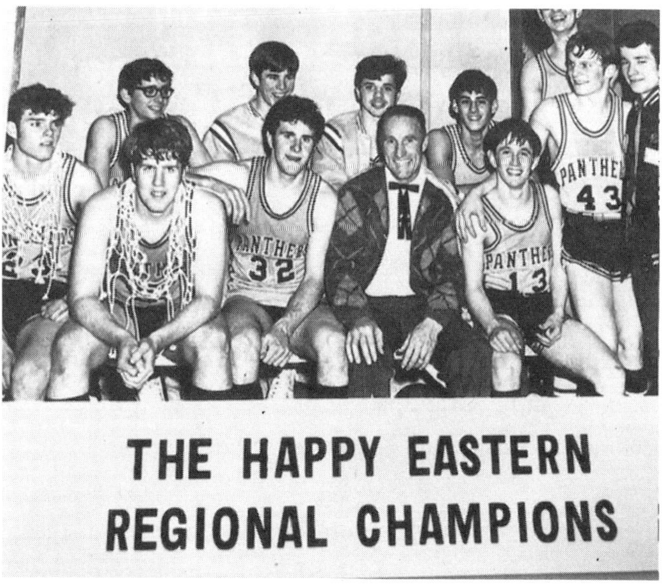

Glennallen boys basketball team in late 1960s. (Photo courtesy of Copper River School District. Glennallen, Alaska.)

As a new staff member, Kenny received his job description.

"I would be teaching Social Studies, History, Government, and PE (physical education) in the classroom. Depending on the sports season, I'd be coaching boys' and girls' basketball, wrestling, and track.

"I had also worked out a plan to attain my Alaska guiding license. Cleo McMahan, an established guide, had agreed I could apprentice with him for three years. The school district was willing to work with me during the guiding season, which ran from August through October. During those months, a substitute teacher would be hired for my classes. When I finished guiding and outfitting, I was in the classroom and able to get the sports programs set for the students. It worked out well for all of us."

With the background Kenny had in basketball, physical training, and politics, he was able to bring life experiences into his interactions with the young people. He was a popular teacher and had a good rapport with the students.

Two of Dan's daughters had some reflections on their grandfather and basketball in Glennallen.

Wendy Sailors said, "Grandpa grew up with a strong woman and had a strong wife. He felt the girls needed a chance to grow strong, be challenged, and play with a real basketball. Not just half-court with a six-girl team and a rubber ball. But full court, where they could play hard. He was proud of his girls! The team paid attention, focused, and did what he instructed them to do and made great strides in their abilities."

Kelly Sailors Gerlach added, "He taught with purpose and passion, showing by example. Grandpa was devoted to growing each girl as an individual and letting them know that he believed in them. Because he did."

In the Jump Shot DVD, Jeannette Tegeler Sutherland, a team member in the 1970s, remembered: "It was something to realize we had a basketball coach who had played in the NBA, for the Boston Celtics, here in our little town of Glennallen."

Kenny spoke with admiration about his girls. "I was especially proud when Margaret Auble became the first player to successfully and correctly shoot the jump shot. The fledgling team of girls in Glennallen became stronger and surer of their skills. Kenny's first year of coaching ended when his girls' team won an invitational tournament they played at the University of Alaska in Fairbanks.

"I made use of what Ev Shelton had taught me," Kenny stated. "I focused on the importance of solid defense and the innovative weave offense. The team did what I told them to do. I always encouraged the girls to work hard and be aggressive on the court but, admonished them to be ladies off the court."

Athabascan player Rose Charley Tyrone had a special recollection of Kenny. In the Jump Shot DVD, she recalled, "I wasn't a very good player. But Coach Sailors must have seen something in me he knew

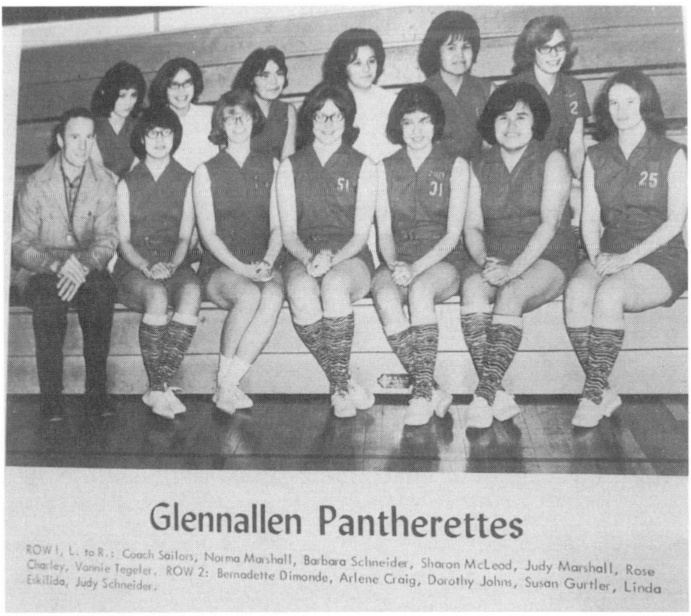

Coach Sailors and a Glennallen girls' basketball team late 1960's.
(Photo courtesy of Copper River School District. Glennallen, Alaska.)

could be developed. He was patient and persistent. I grew because he believed in me and I knew he cared. He did that for all of the players."

From 1965-1974, the Glennallen girls team won three state championships and finished second in a fourth year. Jeannette Tegeler Sutherland told of their amazing run, "We had a winning streak of 68 games."

Kenny explained, "The teams were primarily made up of native kids. There were a few whites on both the girls' and boys' teams who were from the area and the Central Alaskan Mission (CAM) families. I appreciated all of my players."

The native team members impressed Sailors. "Those kids were strong and knew how to work hard as they helped their families bring in food for the coming year. During the salmon run, the gals would work the fish wheels at the river's edge and hang the catch on racks to dry. Dried or smoked salmon is called 'Squaw Candy' and is a staple winter food for rural Alaskans and their dogs.

"Butchering moose or caribou didn't faze those girls either. It was a group effort to get the meat prepared for storage in the caches, where the meat could be frozen in the winter and kept away from animals.

"Getting wood was a huge task. Hauling the downed timber was done using dog sleds if there was snow. If there wasn't snow, the sleds were modified with wheels and the dogs provided the 'foot power' to make the process work.

"Yes, those little ladies knew how to work. They weren't tall, but they were fast and had grit and determination."

About the basketball teams, Kenny said, "You better believe I was on the trot, coaching both girls' and boys' basketball. I'd tape the ankles of the girls' team, then coach their game. A little before the end of that game my helper on the bench would finish up. I'd take off for the boys' locker room and tape up their ankles and we'd all head for the floor. Yes, I was busy, but I loved it. I loved working with those kids."

Chapter 32

GIRLS BASKETBALL IN ALASKA

"Building the girls' team in Glennallen, was the first step in establishing a girls' basketball program in Alaska. There were a few Catholic schools that had girls' basketball teams in the area. However, we needed other girls' teams to play. I began to brainstorm for ways to get other communities interested in girls' basketball."

It may have been a happy coincidence, but the boys' basketball team made the way for Kenny to become an advocate for girls' basketball throughout the state.

"The first year I was in Glennallen, my boys' team was at the state basketball tournament. I made the most of meeting other coaches and players. Chatting with the cheerleaders was a great way to suggest they talk to their school administrators about starting a girls' basketball program for themselves.

"As time went on, I met more basketball folks. I was able to have some of my girls travel with me to make presentations to other schools. We encouraged those coaches to start this new basketball program for their girls. They listened and were interested. The cheerleaders helped spread the word about basketball for girls. Our presentations were successful and the girls' basketball programs began to grow throughout the school districts. No one seemed to be upset that girls were no longer cheering at the boys' games. The young ladies were all playing on basketball teams of their own.

"Once the girls' teams started to get organized, the gals had so much fun playing together that they wanted to be playing basketball in those small schools. Girls' basketball programs began to increase in popularity and grow throughout the public school districts of Alaska."

Kenny even mentioned he was impressed by watching the savvy play of a young Sarah Heath in Palmer, Alaska. Her girls' team went on to win a state championship in 1982. Later she married and went on to become the Mayor of Wasilla and the Governor of Alaska, known as Sarah Palin.

As a coach and a player, Kenny recognized there were many valuable character strengths and attributes that could be developed through a well-balanced sports program.

The Alaska legislature took notice of what Kenny had done with few resources and a lack of funding. His impact on girls' basketball led to the development of other opportunities for young females. The State Legislature issued a special commendation to Kenny Sailors for his efforts to establish girls' basketball in the state of Alaska.

As tax revenue funneled into the state due to the Trans Alaska Pipeline project, Title IX was implemented. Funding became available to advance the opportunities for girls' sports programs statewide.

When the girls' basketball program was solidly in place, Kenny was ready to focus his attention on developing his guiding and hunting business. It turned out to be the right time to transition once again from basketball to the outdoors and guiding.

Chapter 33

THE BUILDER

Kenny had several ideas for building projects in his new home state. But first, he and Boky would build a home for themselves.

"I discovered we could apply for a five-acre Home Site through the Bureau of Land Management, also known as the BLM. We continued to live in the trailer court while we worked on our home.

"Marilynne and I were thankful for our experience of building a log home in Wyoming, back in the 1950s. Our Swedish mentor in Laramie had taught us well. We cleared trees, which were peeled and hewed into shape. The Swede's instructions for dove-tailed corners ensured we had a tight and sturdy building. Our son Dan and Dr. Noonkesser from Faith Hospital at CAM helped with the process. The result was a solid and snug cabin.

"Just down the road from our new cabin was a native church. Ben Neely, a tribal chief, pastored the Gulkana Chapel along with his friend, Fred Ewan. Boky and I attended the chapel and became friends with the men and their wives. They were fine people we enjoyed through the years we lived in the area. Those men had a special impact on my spiritual life as well."

Years later, when Ben Neely was dying, Kenny was at his bedside. It was reported that Ben thanked the coach for giving native girls throughout Alaska the opportunity to participate in basketball and achieve success in that sport.

Kenny continued, "I became involved in Glennallen's American Legion Post. When I learned there were no Boys' State programs in the 49th state, I went to work to remedy that situation. With support from that legion group, I started a Boy's State program for Alaska in 1966.

"With the week-long gathering, we taught high school juniors the fundamental components of American government. Of importance to me was helping young people understand the strength of our Democratic Republic. This form of government has stood the test of time throughout the history of our nation. I felt very strongly about stressing the importance of civic and community involvement on a personal level.

"Students had the opportunity to participate in a mock legislature. Parties were developed and officials were elected to their 'state' government. Bills were composed, discussed, passed, or defeated. The kids loved it and thrived in that new experience. I worked with Alaska Senator Ted Stephens, who conducted the mock Senate. I was in charge of the mock House of Representatives.

"Once again, I was able to use my political experiences to share important concepts with the future leaders of our next generation.

"With my past political experience, several politicians encouraged me to run for office in the 49th state. I ran once and was defeated. That took care of that.

"I had grown because of my election losses. Failing to win a political contest allowed me to be humbled. Character and integrity were positive outgrowths of those experiences and gave credibility to what I had to offer."

Kenny was also working to build his hunting and guiding business. This would be the lynchpin that kept them in Alaska.

"Cleo McMahan allowed me to join him as an assistant guide while I worked to complete the requirements of a hunting guide in Alaska. Even though I had years of experience in Wyoming, I had to work for three years under a licensed Alaska guide. I had to collect recommendations from hunters and pass a written test. If I had a good enough score I'd be able to take an oral test. The big shots were not going to make it easy to become a guide in Alaska. But I did what it took to become a licensed hunting guide."

.....

In the winter of 1967, Kenny's mother died in a Cheyenne convalescent home at the age of eighty-six. At Cora's funeral service in his home state, Kenny gave a heartfelt tribute.

"Mother had a profound spiritual influence on my life. It wasn't just religious pretense. Through the years my mother practiced what she preached. She took us to church. We prayed over meals and lifted our needs to the Lord. At night we read the Bible and discussed how it applied to our lives. She ended her prayers with, 'Not my will, but Thy will be done.'

"My mother knew that God had the best plan. She persevered in faith to get the job done in a way that would honor God. I learned from her.

"We lived by the standards of 'The Golden Rule.' The determination and resolute belief she displayed throughout all the challenges of life had to have come as an outgrowth of a deep, abiding faith she had in God and Jesus Christ. Faith and a relationship with God carried her through all she endured.

"I knew the *benefits* of faith, but it took me a while to make that *profession* of faith. When we ended up in Glennallen, the good folks at the Central Alaska Mission brought the pieces together for me and I accepted Christ as my Savior. Marilynne had been growing in her faith, due to the influence of the Bahu family in San Diego. Now we began growing together as husband and wife.

“My mother and my wife were the two most important influences in my life.”

.....

Kenny was interested in learning about the Alaska Native Claims Settlement Act (ANCSA). In 1971, an act was passed by the United States Congress to settle Indigenous land claims in Alaska. Around 44 million acres of land were transferred to thirteen native, for-profit corporations designed to serve the culture, community, and corporate responsibilities of Alaska Natives. The Athabascans were indigenous to interior Alaska, which included the Glennallen, Gulkana, and Gakona localities.

The Ahtna, Athabascan corporation was formed in the Glennallen area and was composed of one village corporation, twelve communities, and eight tribes. Unlike most corporations, the shares can be given away or inherited, but not sold.

Kenny recalled, “After we proved up on our five-acre homesite, we applied for an eighty-acre ‘homestead’ through the Bureau of Land Management. This would be for the guiding business we planned to establish. That land parcel was one mile west of our first home.

“To prove up on the homestead we had to build a house, live there for a year, and improve the land. We built a lodge for the guiding business and cultivated twenty acres of grass for the horses. By that time Dan was a registered, commercial bush pilot. He and his family lived at that place. Later on, his daughter Kelly and her family would live on the homestead.

“I was tired of teaching at that point and had completed my three years as an assistant to Cleo. I was ready to start my own business at our ‘76 Ranch.’ We had moved from the designation of ‘Cheechako’ to ‘Sourdough.’ Alaska was our home.”

Chapter 34

ALASKA HUNTING GUIDE BUSINESS

"A lot of folks think guiding sounds glamorous," Kenny stated. "I can tell you, it is exciting and interesting. It is also challenging, tough, frustrating, and hard. But once it gets in your blood, there it is. Boky and I loved it. The fresh air, views, and the great outdoors were good for us, especially my wife. The good Lord continued to watch over us. She felt better than she had for a long time.

"When I first got into the hunting guide business in Alaska, most of the guides I spoke with didn't know much about horses. Many of the bush pilots in the state had come up during World War II and stayed in Alaska when they realized they could make a living flying and guiding. In Wyoming, pack horses were a natural part of the operation for me. I liked horses and riding so I decided to keep using them. My hunting partner Cleo was one of the best bush pilots in the business. He eventually got into utilizing horses as well.

"Dan was familiar with horses and liked working with them. But truthfully, he liked being a pilot better. His interest in flying was inspired by Dave Lowe, one of the young fellows who came to the Heart Six ranch, back in Wyoming.

Moose hunt in the Mentasta Mountains. Kenny on the front horse, Chuck McMahan on the third horse, crossing the Tetlin River in the 1980s. (Photo courtesy of Sailors family.)

"Later on, Cleo and his son Harley developed a business farther into the interior of the state around Meirs Lake. Chuck McMahan, another son of Cleo's, took over his dad's partnership with me at that time. The two brothers had been guides for us when I first started. Chuck was a bush pilot, and a good one. He and I worked together well for twenty years.

"It was hard work using horses in Alaska. They ate a lot of feed, and getting them through the extreme winters was tough. I always figured it was worth it though. Clients seemed to thrive on the unique experience horses brought to hunting. Folks from the city discovered how horses changed the pace of their day. There was something therapeutic and comforting about the rhythm of riding. The clink of tack metal and creak of saddle leather seemed to pull individuals into the present moment. For us as guides, those faithful critters made packing out big game animals much easier.

"Nice weather days were unbeatable when we were in the mountains. Miserable days, not so much. When each hunt was done, there was a sense of satisfaction that seemed to make people sit a little taller in the saddle and walk with new confidence."

In a few years, the 76 Ranch was up and running during the autumn. "My wife and I would head 'outside' during mid-winter to escape the freezing temperatures. We used those dark months to attend the outdoor trade shows in the lower forty-eight states. Those events were set up in big cities across the United States, typically held during the off-season for fishing and hunting.

"Marilynne and I would go to the sportsman shows and rent booths to advertise. We always brought antlers to display. Sort of like show and tell for those hunters who dreamed of bagging a *Boone and Crockett* record-breaking trophy.

"Folks were fascinated by Alaska." Kenny shared. "While guiding was hard work, the tradeshows were a fun part of the business. When prospective clients asked about our hunts, I had a variety of stories to share. Some were unbelievable. Some were whacky. Most of them were memorable.

"Our big game hunts were in the Mentasta Mountains, northeast of Glennallen, 65 miles from the Canadian border. Guided horse-back hunts were for Dahl sheep, moose, caribou, grizzly, black bear, wolf, and wolverine. Clients enjoyed staying in our semi-permanent wall tents. These canvas structures had sturdy pole frames, wood stoves and lanterns, typical in guiding operations. Family-style meals were served by the camp cook. This was all part of a once-in-a-lifetime experience for our guests.

"September first of one year, four clients hit the jackpot.

"We had an ordinary arrival with the four men. Supper was served up, we relaxed then settled into our tents. Soon big fat snowflakes commenced to float down upon the peaceful camp. By midnight, the tents were sagging from the weight of the accumulated flakes. Worried the tents would collapse, I woke the guides up to clear snow from the sagging canvas. Even though a supply tent caved in, we were able to save the other structures.

"The next morning, it was a humdinger of an early storm. The cold had set in with nearly two feet of snow on the ground and more coming down. There was no way it was safe to go anywhere. We kept the coffee pot full. There were *Louis L'Amour* books to pass around, 'just in case' we needed some sort of entertainment. And this hunt we did.

"It was rough sledding all the way around. With too much snow and no hunting, everyone in camp was on the peck. It wasn't until the ninth day when the clouds finally broke and the skies began to clear over the rugged mountains. Halleluiah! Camp gloom began to lift.

"By that point, the out-of-staters wondered if they'd ever return home to civilization. I figured we needed to make a two-day extension for this snow-bound hunting expedition.

"With one of those 'amazing miracles' in the mountains when we couldn't get onto the peaks to hunt for sheep, lo and behold! The Dall sheep had descended from their high perches and moved into a nearby valley where they were easy to reach.

"In those two days, you never saw such hunting in your life. Every single one of those guys got a sheep and didn't even have to climb a mountain.

"Now, that was the hunt of an Alaska lifetime for me. Not a grand slam. But it was a dandy."

Kenny always reminded his clients, "I'm here to guide you, but you will be the one to harvest the animal. We'll make sure the meat is properly taken care of and nothing will go to waste. That was an important childhood lesson I had learned. I made it a point to pass it on.

"Our hunters were glad to follow our policy. Each person took care of the horns, cape, and whatever meat they would be taking home. We partnered with Ahtna chief, Ben Neely, to distribute the excess game to his tribal elders and members."

Chapter 35

MISSION AND PIPELINE OPPORTUNITIES

After getting settled in the trailer court in the fall of 1965, Marilynne found work in Glennallen at Faith Hospital, which was a part of the Central Alaska Mission.

Kenny recalled, "It took both of us to make our new venture work. Boky was employed in the CAM (Central Alaska Mission) hospital business office for fifteen years and I was at the school for eight years.

"Marilynne enjoyed working with people over the years. When we had the Women's Convalescent Home in Cheyenne, she and Mother made a great team. Boky liked tending to the ladies and seemed to have the right touch to encourage them.

"At Faith Hospital, Boky's experience was a bonus. She was able to step in and assist where she was needed. I was relieved to know if Marilynne had a breathing problem, she was already at the hospital. I realized during the time in Alaska, my wife was healthier than she had been for some time.

"That is... until the dementia set in. Doctors said the steroids she used in the early years of her life may have contributed to this problem. I guess we'll never know. I do know that we were grateful for the many extra years of life we were able to share.

"Marilynne also loved gardening. We were able to build a large greenhouse for her. With the long summer daylight hours, Boky had quite the garden. Those 19-20-hour summer days of interior Alaska produced incredible vegetables. Believe me, my girl did a great job putting up food for the year."

Granddaughter Wendy Sailors recalled, "Sometimes my sister Kelly and I would stay with Grandma while the rest of the family was out guiding. We loved helping her with the chores. She had a way of making work fun.

"Grandma had a green thumb, then worked hard to store food for the family. She enjoyed sharing canned goods with the Bible College in town. Her energy, efforts, and generosity were greatly appreciated by our family and throughout the community."

After Kenny left teaching in 1974, he sought new opportunities. "On a lark, I figured I'd check out a job with Alyeska Pipeline. I was hired and worked from Prudhoe Bay up north, and down south to Valdez, where the oil terminal was built. I hired on as a payroll clerk and then I moved on to manage a warehouse.

"The pay was good, but I just didn't like being stuck working inside. I heard about the chance to drive a ten-ton truck and I had to join the Teamsters. I was off to hauling rock and gravel. Let me tell you, hauling that material to the pipeline was a big job.

"With construction, there were always a lot of scraps and miscellaneous materials left over. In the beginning, the pipeline company took that stuff to the dump. When the local stores complained about losing business due to people scavenging in the dump, Alyeska decided to burn the dump piles. After the way I grew up, that was a darn hard thing to watch. I understood the other side of the issue though.

"Alyeska built man camps along the pipeline where the workers lived. Our homesite was close by and allowed me to stay at home because of my nearby truck route. I could take a lunch or eat in the mess hall for the crews if I wanted.

"Driving a truck required adjustments on some of the basics of vehicle care. When the temperatures dropped below -40°, we never shut the engines off.

"I went on to drive a bus and transport the pipeline workers to and from the job sites. The company made sure their help had good lunches. Right off the bat, I noticed there were a lot of lunch items tossed into the trash box at the front of my bus. Once again I sure didn't like seeing perfectly good food go to waste.

"After the crews left the bus, I cleaned the vehicle. When that chore was finished, I went through what had been discarded and sorted out what was still good. I took those items home for Boky to work her magic in the kitchen."

Dan remembered, "My mother didn't have any problem recycling from Pop's trash box. It was amazing to see what she could do with those treasures from the front of the bus. Dried, pickled, canned, or made into jam, the food was darn good and freely shared with others."

Kenny reflected on interesting events he had witnessed over his life. Years before, he had seen unusual and unbelievable sights in the big cities. However, remote Alaska hatched some memorable moments that were goofy and unexpected.

"For instance, a Gakona resident worked in the kitchen of a nearby man camp. Always ready for action, Carol was in prime form one Halloween.

"It had been a boring day. Workers were lulled into complacency.

"Suddenly, the back door to the lunchroom burst open. A sheet-covered figure hurtled among the tables. Squawking, squeaking, and flapping. This—this—aberration ran around and finally stopped behind one of the diners. The man dived under the table only to be caught by his arm and pulled up short. To his embarrassment, his darlin' wife pulled off her sheet and planted a big smooch on his kisser!

The lunchroom burst into shouts of glee and laughter. Ho-hum had turned into He-haw.

"You never knew what might show up outside. Ordinary Alaska highways had their share of surprises. One neighbor laughed about a drive they had from Anchorage to Gakona. As they crested a hill leaving the Matanuska Valley near Palmer, a purse was spotted on the right shoulder of the road. The couple wondered if there had been an accident, or something worse. Russ figured he'd better have a little look-see.

"He hopped out of the truck and walked around the back while his wife watched. She saw her husband step over the edge of the road and disappear into the brush.

"He finally re-emerged from the tangled bushes, laughing.

"When Russ opened the pickup door, he said, 'You are not going to believe this! The purse was tied to a string that led into the brush where two kids were hidden. There they crouched, laughing their heads off.'"

Even in remote areas of the 49th state, folks had a sense of humor and enjoyed some good old-fashioned fun.

Kenny looked back over his years working on the pipeline. "When that wrapped up, I taught classes at Central Alaska Bible College in Glennallen for a time. I figured I could spend more time fishing and hunting.

"I just didn't figure on more Alaska surprises."

Chapter 36

ANGOON

Kenny Sailors should have known better.

In 1987, a man from Central Alaska Mission came to Kenny with a proposal.

"Kenny," he started. "I have a friend down on Admiralty Island who is the Superintendent of the school district. Angoon is about 55 miles southwest of Juneau. He's got discipline issues with the junior high students and needs a girls' basketball coach. Would you consider talking with him?"

Kenny paused. "Let me talk to Marilynne and pray about it."

"Returning to teaching and coaching was not on my mind, but Boky and I agreed to check out southeast Alaska.

"The school flew us to Angoon for an interview. Marilynne immediately fell in love with the coastal setting of the Tlingit village. We were struck by the beauty of the area.

"Sea level was good for Marilynne. She liked the thought of living on the coast. The superintendent knew we were in the guiding business, and he made sure to highlight opportunities that included fishing and hunting. The view of the glistening waters of nearby Chatham Strait was beautiful.

"That guy was no dummy. He knew where our 'sweet spot' was. When he tossed out the offer, we caught his pass. I promised to give him one year as both a basketball coach and a school teacher.

"We returned to Gakona to prepare for the move. At age sixty-seven, I was slowing down. Dan was ready to shift from time in the saddle to more time in the cockpit of his Super Cub. He pursued his flying interests as a bush pilot. From then on, Chuck McMahan had the hunting guide business. Marilynne and I headed to Admiralty Island.

"The school district provided a comfortable four-room apartment for us. It was easy to walk where we needed to go. However, we did need to get used to the *bear bell.*

"When a bear was sighted, a bell started to ring. There might have been more bears than people in the Angoon area. At the toll of the bell, residents learned they needed to 'high tail it' into a building until the bear(s) had left."

Because of the many intimidating omnivores on Admiralty Island, Kenny and Marilynne had to get creative with a conditioning plan for the girls' basketball team.

"Marilynne and I drove alongside the girls as they ran on the dump road. I called out encouragement as my wife rode shotgun. Literally. She sat with a loaded shotgun at the ready, in case a bear appeared. Thankfully, we never had to discharge a slug from 'old Bessy' the shotgun. Marilynne was honored by the girls, who affectionately named her, 'the dump road queen.'"

On the first day of school, Kenny wasn't sure what to expect. "The superintendent had informed me that along with the junior high discipline problems, he and the principal did not see eye-to-eye."

"Kenny," the boss said, "Do what you think is best to handle situations you encounter. Don't hesitate to come to my office. I'll back you up."

"I headed off to my first class, a group of seventh graders. Two girls had exchanged words before I arrived. As I entered the room, one gal was thumping another gal who had mouthed off to her. The two of them were thrashing around on the floor. I scrambled through kids and desks, to find the girl on the floor being walloped.

"I pushed my way to the dogpile and hoisted the attacker up. I wasn't sure what to do. My goal was to keep her away from the struggling student on the floor.

"I held her out in front of me as I threaded my way through the desks, out the door, and down the hall to the principal's office. Once inside the room, I sat her down in a chair.

The Principal looked at me with his eyes bugged out. 'What's going on here?' he barked.

"Before I could answer, the Principal asked the student, 'Now, did coach hurt you?'"

The girl stiffened and spat out, "Yes, under my arms."

The administrator looked at the student. "I'm calling your mother."

"That's fine with me," Kenny stated.

When her mother arrived, "the young gal made a fuss," Kenny recalled.

"I told the mother what I had encountered. The next thing I knew, she backhanded her daughter and nearly knocked her off her chair."

"What the heck did you think you were doing?" the mother demanded. "Why would you do such a thing?"

"I was surprised," Kenny said, "when the mother grabbed her daughter by the arm and marched her out the door.

"I suppose it was her action that saved me. Plus, the fact that the Superintendent said I had his support.

"It was several days before the student returned to school. The Principal told her she had to behave. After that, her attendance was sporadic. I always felt bad to realize what her home life must have been like."

"After that first day, I had no problems. Those kids just needed somebody who cared enough to call their bluff."

There were only thirty-seven students in grades nine through twelve. To have fifteen girls out for his team was a credit to Kenny's enthusiasm and interest. There was no doubt he was committed to helping his team learn and improve. Folks were quick to recall the time a player suffered an ankle injury. Coach ran to the girl, picked her up, and carried her from the floor.

The girls' basketball team in Angoon ended up on a winning path in southeast Alaska. The team listened to their coach as he taught them to use their natural talents and skills. They developed a strong offense and established a tough defense. The team went on to win a big prize, the conference championship. This was a very big deal in southeast Alaska where competition was extremely stiff.

Sailors said, "I felt the girls' team would have won another championship but a key player suffered a broken wrist at the state tournament. She had no replacement, which was a disappointment. Regardless, I was very proud of them. In 1990, the girls placed fourth in the championships."

Students said, "Coach helped us to believe in ourselves. We grew and succeeded because he believed in us."

"The Angoon basketball team had many success stories. Several girls went on to play university ball and graduated with degrees. Others went on to raise families and contribute to the communities and businesses where they lived. Kenny and his wife were proud of them all. The community was proud of them.

The Sailors had developed genuine relationships and came to be highly regarded in the community of Angoon. School administrators, staff, and townspeople considered Kenny "a treasure."

Kenny remarked, "By state law, I had to retire from teaching at age 70. At the end of three years, our adventure on Admiralty Island had finished. Marilynne and I returned to Gakona and a quiet life."

Or so they thought.

Chapter 37

NEXT SEASON OF LIFE

Before Marilynne and Kenny left Angoon, she had something to say on a subject she'd been thinking about.

"Corn Tassel, we're going to go to Arizona to start hunting rattlesnakes."

"Hunting rattlesnake?"

Kenny's girl was not kidding. "I'm looking forward to getting to Arizona to spend time in that dry, desert heat."

Kenny had to admit, "Warm weather doesn't sound that bad. Rattlesnakes? That could be another deal. Remember snakes are out of their latitude limits in Alaska. Except for a garter snake or two."

Boky responded. "Oh fiddlesticks, you can hunt anything you put your mind to."

Scratching his Marine haircut, Kenny shrugged. "Guess I'll work on that idea."

"My brother and his wife had sold the Heart Six Ranch in Wyoming and moved to Wickenburg, Arizona. On some of our business trips outside, we visited them and enjoyed the Grand Canyon State. Bud and I found we still had much in common despite how circumstances had changed us. We liked being able to spend time together in a quiet and unpressured environment. Boky and I decided to consider moving south permanently.

"The next year, Marilynne's memory problems continued to grow worse."

Granddaughter Wendy recalled, "Sometimes Grandma would be fixing a meal for the two of them and have the table set for ten. It was sad to see what was going on, but we would love on her, laugh and joke along with her. She was such a source of joy and encouragement."

Kenny began to notice more lapses in daily routines with his girl.

"At night, I'd wake up and realize she wasn't next to me. I'd check the usual spots in the house, find her, and bring her back to bed.

"One winter night I woke up. She wasn't in bed and I checked the regular places. Not in the bathroom. Not in the kitchen. The only other place to look was outside. Outside…It was probably -30° or -40°.

"I headed through the front door and found her away from the house, in her nightclothes, standing in the snow. There she was, gazing up into the splendor of the arctic night surrounded by the Northern Lights.

"Boky and I loved to go out and watch those lights. Often, we could hear a couple of owls hooting back and forth. Or we would hear a pack of wolves yapping and howling off in the distance. It was nature's music to our ears."

The Aurora Borealis is a truly spectacular phenomenon of the far northern sky. This light show is produced by charged electrons and protons striking gas particles in the upper atmosphere of the earth. Sunspots also factor into the activity.

Colors blossom in shades of green, red, blue, and purple. The lights occur in patterns that move and undulate across the inky sky. Some people say the sound of the Aurora makes a noise similar to rustling taffeta fabric. Others say the sounds are eerie or ethereal.

"We loved the sounds of the outdoors. As the waves of color shimmered and moved through the heavens, the effect was breathtaking.

On occasion, the bands of color seemed to swoop down to meet a mere human in a glorious, mantle of brilliance.

"That particular night, Boky seemed to be wrapped in a lovely arctic shawl. I moved over to gather her into my arms and hold her close. The majesty of God's creation followed us as we turned and traced our footsteps back into the warmth of our log cabin.

"I knew the time had come to have a talk with our friends at Faith Hospital."

His doctor was serious. "Kenny, it's time to think about getting Marilynne to a safer place to live. You don't know when she will wander outside and not be found until it is too late."

"He was right. The arctic cold is nothing to trifle with.

"I talked to my brother Bud about Marilynne's situation. He had a house at his Arizona place that he would sell to us when the time was right. We traveled to Wickenburg in 1991 to see what we could work out.

"We spent that winter in the Grand Canyon state and found the climate agreed with us.

"I figured I would learn to deal with rattlesnakes.

"Bud and Betty sold us their extra house. Wickenburg became our winter residence for several years. We enjoyed the summers in the Copper River Valley of Alaska and continued to return to our log cabin at Gakona as a break from the Arizona heat."

Kenny and Marilynne enjoying their yard at the cabin near Gakona in the 1980s. (Photo courtesy of the Sailors family.)

Chapter 38

TRANSITION

Kenny had disappeared from the national basketball scene when he and Marilynne headed north in 1965. They came as cheechakoes to Alaska with plans to become seasoned residents and established guides. Thirty-four years later, they left as sourdoughs to return to their home state of Wyoming in 1999.

"We hadn't given much thought to the fact that statehood had come to Alaska in 1959, only six years before we arrived. In Seward's Icebox, there wasn't an emphasis on the political, business, or sports activities that were gaining attention in the lower forty-eight.

"Professional basketball was an unknown commodity in the fledgling 49th state and I was fine with that. What I wanted to focus on was building a guiding business. To be off the grid was just dandy with me.

"We had a fairly basic life in the Copper River Valley, north of 60°s of latitude. That is until I started coaching basketball at Glennallen. When Boky mentioned to our friend Daphne I had played for the Boston Celtics, my personal basketball background began to emerge. By the time I was coaching in Angoon, I was getting quite a few questions about the jump shot."

Sailors had written to Lew Freedman, the Sports Editor of the *Anchorage Times,* about his girls' basketball team in Angoon. Freedman picked up the ball and ran with it, writing various articles and two books about the veteran of the hardwood. Those articles became the fodder for the grist mills of sports research and history. Kenny Sailors was rediscovered.

.....

In 1990, Denver hosted the NCAA Final Four with a "Salute to Rocky Mountain Basketball" planned. What do you know? Sleuth work had turned up the fact that jump shot developer Kenny Sailors was "fit as a fiddle" coaching in Angoon, Alaska. Organizers of the event went to great lengths to track down the gent behind the jump shot.

Who?

Was where?

Kenny chuckled as he told of the hullabaloo.

"These big shots made arrangements to fly me to Denver, put me up in a four-star hotel, gave me tickets for the games, and then told me they wanted me to speak!

"I had a whale of a time speaking to a crowd of about twelve hundred basketball supporters during the banquet. Former President Gerald Ford was even there. I just told the group stories of windmills, coaches who inspired me, my basketball-sized girlfriend, my mother who could shoot (but not baskets), and the incredible mythical world championship game we won in 1943.

"I shared how I used the head of a teammate to make two points. Why I taught high school players the 'Shelton Weave,' and the jump shot. My best story might have been about my wife Boky, who was nicknamed the 'queen of the dump road' along with 'old Bessy,' the shotgun.

"Jimmy Reese, my other surviving teammate of the UW 1943 championship team was in attendance in Denver as well. We had a great time recalling who set a pick for whom, how we worked Shelton's offense, and why it worked so well. I think we surprised some of the younger folks with our recollections of the past. The crowd laughed with us as we told about remembering game details from decades ago but probably couldn't find our cars out in the parking lot."

The crowd young and old delighted in the commentary of the jump shot legend. Folks sat up in their chairs and leaned forward to listen as Kenny regaled them with the exploits of his girls on the Alaska basketball courts. Coach wanted those special gals in the spotlight.

Overnight, basketball land responded to the reappearance of the aging cager. Long after the initial Madison Square Garden photograph burst into the news in 1946, interest in the jump shot seemed to take off once again. Sailors found himself back in pictures. This time, as a seventy-year-old girls' coach, standing next to a bigger-than-life poster of his twenty-five-year-old self, set up in a Denver bank lobby.

The Basketball Alumni Foundation named Kenny Sailors one of the "100 Greatest Players of the First Century of Basketball." As a fundraiser, the foundation partnered with a marketing group to produce a set of basketball cards to raise assistance for former league participants who were facing hard times. Sailors was included in that set of cards.

The Alumni Foundation card was not the first collectible card Kenny had appeared on. In 1948, the Bowman Gum Company had produced a set of cards for pro basketball teams. As a member of the Providence Steamrollers, Kenny was on a card in that collection.

A young Alaskan, Ken Johns, was very proud to have been one of Sailors players from his former coaching days in Glennallen. The former high school player had been able to acquire one of those early cards, showcasing former coach Sailors.

Kenny had a humble response. "You know, I never thought all of this stuff was a big deal. I guess it was a big deal. The whole experience resulted in something I never saw coming."

Chapter 39

HUNTING FOR HOME

Kenny remembered, "When we returned from southeast Alaska to our cabin near the Gulkana River, Boky and I thought we would just settle back into a routine life. We figured we would bask in the warmth of Arizona winters and delight in Alaska summers."

All too soon, forgetfulness and unusual incidents began to plague Marilynne's days. When Kenny had checked with doctors at Faith Hospital, it was determined that her early symptoms of Alzheimer's would only complicate the health problems she already had.

"Due to Boky's failing health, we decided to sell our cabin and leave Gakona permanently in 1999. We needed to figure out where home would be for us. Casper, Wyoming, seemed like a good place to get our bearings and figure out the next step. Casper was where she had grown up, and her brother Milton still lived in their hometown."

In the Copper Valley area, it was common for residents to post a message on the bulletin board of the Central Alaska Mission radio station in Glennallen. *Caribou Clatters* was a service program of KCAM radio, *The Voice of the Copper River Valley,* where folks could get all the news of their area. Aired four times a day, the messages reached folks with or without two-way communications.

This popular program was listened to by everybody and their sled dogs. *Clatters* provided a final goodbye message from Corn Tassel and Boky, to their long-time friends and neighbors.

The return trip outside to the lower forty-eight was much different than the first journey to the unknowns of the 49th state. This time they were returning to the familiar "Cowboy State," with many unknowns yet to be faced.

The couple settled down in Casper. It didn't take Kenny long to become involved in basketball programs for younger students through the city recreation department. He enjoyed his time with the kids. Marilynne, on the other hand, enjoyed Corn Tassel and her brother but was not faring well. She was deteriorating faster than they could have imagined.

In 2000, Linda called from Idaho. "Dad, I'd like for you and Mom to come live with me, so I can help you take care of her."

Kenny recalled, "Some years before, we had purchased a small place out of Gooding, Idaho, for Linda. It seemed like a good idea to take her up on the offer. We moved west to be with our daughter and be nearer her children.

"Boky continued to lose ground after we moved. Unexpected situations came up where she locked doors and kept people out, or turned stove burners on and didn't shut them off. My girl needed more home care than Linda and I could give her. We looked for an alternate situation and found a wonderful assisted care facility for her.

"The inevitable had come. Linda and I moved Boky about fifteen miles to Shoshone, Idaho. My heart broke as we took her to the new place, but I knew she would be safe. We could visit her regularly.

"I thought back to Mrs. Bahu in San Diego. How that dear persecuted Palestinian Christian had shared the gift of eternal life with my girl and led Marilynne to accept Jesus as her Savior. There was no doubt in my mind where both of those ladies would be. I knew I could look forward to seeing them again in eternity.

"Boky died on April 13, 2002. Her body was buried in the Gooding cemetery, but her soul was now free.

"You know, early in our marriage, doctors said Marilynne would be lucky if she lived to see fifty years of age. By changing our lifestyle, my girl lived another 28 years we didn't think we'd have. I was grateful to God."

Granddaughter Wendy reflected, "Grandma had stayed with Grandpa through all of his adventures. They loved each other immensely and were devoted to each other."

Devotion was a word that not only family members used to describe the relationship that Kenny and Marilynne had. Friends, neighbors, and the scores of young people Kenny had encouraged over the years echoed that very same word. Devoted. To God and each other.

Kenny was thoughtful. "This journey hasn't been easy. We are told in God's Word that when we do our part, we can count on God. He gives us the strength to get through what comes along in life.

"After my girl was gone," Kenny reflected, "I stayed on with Linda in Gooding for three years. We helped each other as we moved on in life. I joked that I could be her retired farm laborer for a time."

He did the farm gig for a spell then decided to try a move to Laramie. Kenny's nephew and wife helped him relocate to Laramie and settle in a place near them.

When that didn't work out, he found an apartment closer to the university and sports doings. He found opportunities for group engagements, making new acquaintances, and reconnecting with old friends.

In town, he began to attend the Laramie Community Recreation Center. Meeting people was not a problem for Kenny Sailors. He would start up a conversation with any unsuspecting gym rat who happened to be parked beside him. The circle of friends and activities grew.

Danny Nelson, Rick Stuart, and Bill Schrage met Kenny through activities at the REC center. Those three fellows had good times together with Kenny and were able to lend a hand if he needed one. Over the many years, Kenny had been the person willing to help others. As life has a way of changing circumstances, this trio now pitched in and volunteered when Kenny had tasks that needed to be done.

A highly respected Laramie teacher known for his hospitality, Danny Nelson brought folks together for meals and drew Kenny into a welcoming fellowship.

Danny recalled, "I decided I could plan a weekly meal to socialize with Kenny and other folks I knew. One thing led to another and I began to help my new friend with issues that were driving him crazy. Kenny was ready to throw in the towel on technology because his phone went haywire. Then his insurance paperwork got out of hand. I was glad to step in and ease the burden. We finally got those miserable deals figured out. Believe me, it was an ordeal!"

Rick Stuart was a retired ranch cowboy who happened to sit down next to Kenny at a Cowgirls basketball game in the Arena.

Kenny glanced over, "Well, hello there young fella."

How could Rick resist that invitation? The two men settled down into their stadium seats and commenced to compare horse stories. It was a fine way to watch basketball and chew the fat regarding time spent in the saddle.

Rick reminisced, "The REC center was another place Kenny and I would meet for workouts. Eventually, we became roommates and helped each other out for a couple of years. A favorite activity for us would be to have impromptu Bible studies. We could talk for hours about scriptures. Then we'd go out to eat."

Another guy who frequented the REC center was Bill Schrage. He recalled, "The first time Kenny and I met, we talked about Jesus Christ. We didn't even introduce ourselves we just had a conversation about the Lord. The next time we met, basketball dominated the conversation. Finally, we decided to introduce ourselves. What a relief to know who we'd been talking with."

Wyoming native John Faulkner became another great friend from the REC center. He was introduced to Kenny by his stepson Dusty Joy. The fellows ended up having spaghetti together at Dusty's house. As it turned out, Kenny was fond of the signature Italian dish and was a good reason for the group of friends to gather on a regular basis.

A former acquaintance reappeared in Kenny's life in 2005. Vance Burch was the sixteen-year-old boy from the 1950s who had hunted at the Heart Six Ranch. Vance had moved to Laramie and was attending an "All-Century" game in the UW Fieldhouse, which Kenny was a part of. During the celebration activities, he caught Kenny's attention.

"Kenny," Vance called out. "I was hunting at the Heart Six back in the 1950s. I had that special hunting knife."

Stopping to shake Vance's hand, Kenny looked him in the eye. "I remember that knife. I'll give you my phone number. Let's talk later."

Vance recalled, "He did, we met, we talked, and then we decided we were hungry."

"I've got a moose roast," offered Kenny, "let's go to the store to pick up what we need to make a meal."

Vance continued, "We took off to shop, cook and visit. We even found out we were both Marines. Old leathernecks like to stick together you know. That was the beginning of a great friendship. We took in available sporting events and participated in Marine activities. When Kenny learned my son Jack was a Marine, he included him in our circle."

Roger and Pat McMicheal came to know Kenny through common friends who were outdoor enthusiasts and hunters with like-minded values. When challenges arose with Veterans benefits for Kenny, Roger was able to get the details taken care of and take the pressure off the old Marine.

Within this group, the friends described Kenny as a person of character and integrity, well-read, and very interested in keeping up with current events. To a person, they were all moved by the love and devotion he freely spoke of regarding Marilynne. Those folks all agreed

Kenny wasn't perfect, but he genuinely cared about folks of all ages and encouraged them in any way he could.

In the early spring of 2011, Kenny hit another road bump in life. He learned Linda was not well and made plans to return to Idaho to assist her.

"When I decided to return to Gooding," Kenny mused, "I didn't know what to expect. It just seemed like I should be there. Over time I've found when opportunities arise, I need to pay attention. This was one of those times. My friends in Laramie helped me pack up and away we went. I was back in Gooding on April 15, 2011.

"My daughter was quite sick, but she didn't want to bother her kids. She kept hiding her symptoms. Finally, in July, a doctor's visit confirmed that she had stage four cancer. I continued to do what I could for her, but it was hard. She finally let her family know she had terminal cancer.

"I recalled lessons from my mother. She never whined or complained. She prayed to God and then trusted the Lord would direct her path. I found strength in doing the same things. That was just the way it was in our lives."

Carrie, Linda's oldest daughter, said, "We had no idea what had been going on with Mom's health or that Grandpa had been taking care of her for several months. When we did find out, my brothers and sister and I stepped in to do what was needed.

"I think Grandpa was overwhelmed and worn out by the ordeal. Fatigue, sadness, and emotions were a difficult combination. People in our family didn't talk about their feelings, so communication was a challenge. He may not have been able to deal with the prospect of losing another daughter. The first part of September, Grandpa abruptly decided to leave Gooding, and returned to Laramie."

Kenny's daughter died six weeks later. He and his son Dan both attended the funeral in Gooding, Idaho, and returned home: Kenny to Laramie and Dan to Aniak, Alaska.

Dan said, "After Mom and Linda died, it seemed like the Lord still had things for Pops to do. Basketball was certainly something he had experience and interest in. Laramie seemed to be calling him back for a different season in basketball."

Chapter 40

HOME IN LARAMIE

Kenny's new group of friends from Laramie had turned up in Gooding to support him in the loss of his daughter. This band of exercise enthusiasts, breakfast pals, and sports followers wanted to show their friend how much he was cared for. And he appreciated it.

When Kenny returned to Laramie the second time, he knew he was home. The old veteran decided he could be picky about where he wanted to set up housekeeping.

After a short stay at Spring Winds Assisted Care Facility in the city, the former Cowboy basketball player moved into an apartment across the parking lot from the Fieldhouse. "I figured I wasn't getting any younger so I might as well situate myself where I'd be close to my favorite activities. Of course, that would be the Arena for basketball activities and the University football stadium.

"It was quite handy. I could go over, walk the concourse of the arena for exercise, watch practice or games, and talk to the new generation of basketball players."

The old cager made a point to talk with both the UW men's and women's basketball teams. Always polite and humble, he never missed an opportunity to listen to kids of all ages and answer their questions or give an autograph. The folks loved him.

People around Kenny appreciated the old-timer as well. One day his neighbor, Hilary Carlson, was locked out of her apartment. Kenny noticed her fussing around and invited her to his place until she could be rescued.

A junior forward on the UW women's basketball team at the time, Hilary gratefully had this to say: "Kenny is a big deal here in Wyoming, but to me, he's just really cool."

Sailors wasn't concerned about being famous or cool. He wanted to reach out to others around him, in ways to serve his Lord and Savior.

Larry Shyatt, then coach of UW Cowboys basketball, said, "As Kenny wandered the halls of the arena, he always made time to talk to students, joke, and answer questions they had. When a team would win, he'd be there to hug and encourage them. When a team lost, he'd be there to hug and encourage them. We have been so fortunate to have the experience of having him around. Kenny had the attitude that whatever you give, comes back 100-fold."

"Basketball has done a lot for me. I want to give back to the community around me."

Other folks would say, "He's got it backward. Kenny has done a lot for basketball." In all humility, Kenny would discount such a statement. He would state, "I'm not famous, it's that stupid jump shot that's famous."

Countless people on and off the court expressed their appreciation for this old Marine jarhead and veteran of basketball. He just plain cared for people.

Over nearly a century, Kenny had a long list of accomplishments. Bill Schrage decided it would be valuable to chronicle the life of the legendary ball player. He stepped into the role as the Kenny Sailors historian in Laramie and enlisted the help of archivist John Waggener at the American Heritage Center (AHC) on the UW campus. Together they created the "Kenny Sailors' Collection" at the AHC.

Chapter 41

RECOGNITION

After attending the 1990 NBA shindig in Denver, Kenny was flooded with an increased number of inquiries about his basketball background and history of the jump shot.

A group of friends in Laramie and around the country began to lobby for Kenny Sailors to be added to the Naismith Basketball Hall of Fame. He figured he'd just let the whole thing play out as it would. He was not interested in talking about himself.

No longer involved in teaching or basketball, Kenny heard from many folks interested in his jump shot. He saw himself as a farm kid who thought up a solution to solve a problem he had faced. "Eventually, I realized I had come up with a different type of basketball shot that worked," he said. "I had simply developed a new way to score on the hardwood."

Agreeing with historians, Sailors said, "It's impossible to find the first person who took a jump shot."

He never claimed to be that player. What set Kenny's jump shot from others was that his new shot showed up on center stage in Madison Square Garden.

Bobby Knight came to meet Kenny in person when he was doing color commentary for a sports newscast in Laramie in 2015. (Photo courtesy of Bill Schrage.)

When interviewed for the 2020 *Jump Shot* documentary, legendary Indiana coach Bobby Knight got a first-time look at the famous jump shot picture of 1946. He stated. "I've never seen this picture before. I want a copy of it." Coming from Knight, that was a high compliment.

To follow up on the Hall of Fame request for Kenny, a group of supporters put together an incredible nomination packet of information that was submitted to the Naismith Hall of Fame Committee to consider Kenny Sailors to be selected to the prestigious group in 2012.

When it was all said and done, Kenny was not in the class of inductees for 2012. The disappointment was sharp. Many of his advocates reasoned that Sailors had disappeared from basketball for too long. He had been forgotten and left behind as the sport advanced over several decades. New players had moved into more prominent positions of development in the sport. His name had simply been lost in the annals of time.

When friends would lament the fact that Kenny should be in the Naismith, he reminded folks, "Of course I'm human. To be in the Naismith Hall of Fame would be an accomplishment. On the other hand, I know I am in a Hall of Fame which is more important. That Hall of Fame has only one person on the selection committee. That would be the Lord."

The crucible of life had refined the purpose and focus of Kenny Sailors.

Sailors had received numerous accolades and achievements throughout his storied career. Those achievements were nice, but when it was all said and done, he knew he would be taking nothing with him at the end.

Instead of resting on his laurels, what did he do? He kept making the most of the opportunities that came his way.

An unexpected phone call set the old cager up for a special finish to his life.

Chapter 42

FINAL PLAY

Located 146 miles northeast of Laramie is a town called Guernsey, Wyoming, a rather unlikely spot for Kenny Sailors to develop a fan club.

The ninety-one-year-old Wyoming Cowboy alum was starting to slow down. In the spring of 2012, Sailors decided to leave his apartment and move into the Spring Winds Assisted Living Facility in Laramie once again. He settled into his new space. His phone was even in working order, thanks to the efforts of his friend Danny Nelson.

Soon after moving, he received a phone call from Troy Reichert, a teacher and coach at Guernsey-Sunrise High School.

"Mr. Sailors. I've got a big, lazy basketball player named Brian who is in summer school. He has an assignment for an English class that requires an interview with a famous Wyoming person. When he googled names, he found that you had developed the jump shot. As a basketball player, that caught his attention. Could we come to Laramie to visit with you?"

Kenny was delighted. "Of course. Let's set up an appointment."

"When Mr. Reichert came," Kenny recalled, "he brought Brian Steiner along with his daughter, Lakin Reichert. We had a nice visit, discussed questions, and had a picture together. Before leaving, the kids asked if there would be a chance their basketball teams could make a trip down to spend a little time with me. How about that?"

Brian returned home to Guernsey, excited about meeting the Wyoming basketball legend. The big, lazy basketball player could not wait to get to work on his assignment. Even though he was nervous, Brian was confident in what he had heard and learned. The meeting with Kenny was to be pivotal in the student's life. Brian had no idea where his research would go. But, it was about to take off.

Within weeks, the Viking basketball teams headed down to Laramie to have a get-together with their rediscovered sports hero. Arrangements were made for the combined Guernsey-Sunrise teams to meet with Kenny in the concourse of the Arena-Auditorium on the UW campus. Kenny took them on a tour of the facility and attended a Cowboys basketball game with the group.

The students quickly bonded with the veteran player and Kenny was genuinely interested in the young athletes. He had plenty of questions for them and kept them engaged in conversation. Enthusiasm ran high.

The Guernsey-Sunrise students with Kenny in the Arena-Auditorium on the UW campus. 2013. (Photo courtesy of Bill Schrage.)

A few weeks later, Kenny received another call from the Vikings coach.

"Hello Mr. Sailors," came the voice of Troy Reichert. "The students are wondering if you would consider being the keynote speaker at the Guernsey-Sunrise spring athletic award ceremony?"

Without missing a beat, Kenny Sailors said, "Why of course I would."

What a thrill for the students to know he would be their event speaker. What excitement for the community to know their own Wyoming basketball great, Kenny Sailors, would come to their small high school with only 72 students.

On the appointed day, Bill Schrage, Danny Nelson, and a friend Ruth Hanks, accompanied Kenny to the Guernsey-Sunrise High School. The former Cowboy star gave a keynote fit for the Hall of Fame. The girls' team presented him with a basketball autographed by each member, complete with nicknames. Kenny's smile beamed his thanks.

The athletic shindig was a success indeed. The attendance count for "the community sports event of the year" far eclipsed what it had ever been previously. The basketball star of yesteryear and his traveling companions did not return home to Laramie until very late that evening. Now that, was quite a deal!

In 2014, the girls of the G-S team made two more visits to spend time with their special friend in Laramie. The teams continued to make more visits to see Kenny during 2015. Those kids had grown to love this old fella, and he loved them back.

Brian Steiner could have been speaking for young people throughout the decades when he stated: "Kenny listened to us kids and made everyone feel comfortable. We knew that he cared and believed in us. He challenged us to do our best and make a difference in the lives of others. Kenny frequently reminded us that there was life beyond sports, through the power of faith in a risen Lord. Kenny Sailors inspired me to elevate my dreams and reach out to others, as he had reached out to me."

Dan Sailors had recognized a profound change that had occurred in his father.

"For Pops to be able to respond to others with such emotion and caring, was something different for our family. We had not learned to deal with emotions, so this was a watershed moment for us. Life has a way of changing people, and the time came when Pops was humbled. Healing had come to him after all he had endured and missed out on in his early life. We saw something special in the way he connected with people, the youth especially. His faith grew, he changed and he finished the game of life, well beyond where he started."

When news was relayed to the Guernsey-Sunrise girls on January 30, 2016, that their friend Kenny had died, there was no question what they would do. They would be at his funeral.

Their school policy stated they would have to take an unexcused absence to attend the affair. The entire team decided they would make the trip. Because the funeral was scheduled for a Friday, the school policy also stated that if sports players missed school the day before a game, they could not play in the game. They would have to forfeit the two week-end games.

Weighing all of the consequences, the girls talked to their parents and the parents talked with the school administration. The girls' team would take the unexcused absences and forfeit the games. Those young ladies would go to Laramie for the funeral of their friend.

Overnight, Wyoming's winter weather changed their plans. Snow and high winds hit the state between Guernsey and Laramie. The Highway Department closed I-80 and roads throughout southeastern Wyoming. No travel was possible. The heartbroken students stayed home and attended their classes.

Pat and Roger McMicheal of Laramie decided it was important to highlight the special relationship Kenny had with this amazing group of small-town students. The couple assembled memorabilia the young people had given to Kenny. The display emphasized a life that rose above difficulty and desperation, to one that succeeded and flourished. People of all ages were touched by a life elevated by faith, character, and integrity.

There could have been no finer finish to a life well lived.

The jump shot of Kenny Sailors changed the world of basketball.

The life of Kenny Sailors changed the world of the people he encountered.

ACKNOWLEDGEMENTS

Thank you to Dan Sailors as he listened to my idea of a project on the life of his dad beyond basketball. Dan gave me contact information for Bill Schrage in Laramie, Wyoming, who had taken on the role of historian for Kenny Sailors. These two men have been the linchpins for bringing this book to life.

To become more informed on Kenny's life, I obtained the "Jump Shop" DVD by Jake Hamilton and took notes during the numerous times I viewed the documentary. I acquired books: *The Origins of the JUMP SHOT*, by John Christgau; *Facts About Alaska,* The Alaska Almanac 15th Edition; *JUMP SHOT,* by Lew Freedman; *Rise and Fire*, by Shawn Fury; *Crossing Alaska;* Essays, by Michelle A. Gilders; *HILLSDALE HERITAGE,* by the Hillsdale Homemakers; *Hunting the Wild Country,* by Kenny Sailors and Lew Freedman; *The Facts* Trans Alaska pipeline system, booklet; COWBOY UP, by Ryan Thorburn. I poured over the volumes, reading the pages and taking copious notes.

Bill sent me the link to the American Heritage Center (AHC) on the University of Wyoming campus. The Kenny Sailors collection contains twenty-two audio files with over twenty-five hours of recorded oral history. Bill Schrage and archivist John Waggener had created an interview outline and posed questions for Kenny to answer and expand upon this resource. I spent scores of hours listening to the sound of Kenny's voice describing his life. With the notes I compiled from hearing his first-person accounts and information from the books, I created a framework for this narrative non-fiction work.

Personal recollections by Kenny's son Dan added depth and value to the work. Dan also made it possible for me to talk to his daughters, Wendy and Kelly, as well as his niece Carrie, the oldest child of his sister Linda. The three girls recalled experiences of special times with their grandparents.

To bring the many threads of the story together, I made several trips to Laramie. Passing through the sweeping rangeland of eastern Wyoming, I pondered what life would have been like more than one hundred years ago.

The farmstead where Kenny spent his early years was near Cheyenne. Through the various seasons, I encountered the sun, the rain, the snow, and the wind, similar to what the Sailors family may have experienced. Oh, that never-ending wind.

Pausing at the summit of I-80 on the high plateau east of Laramie, the screaming gales threatened to tear my hair out as I stepped from the car. (Maybe it was the wind that had made the Colorado coach Frosty Cox cry his eyes out when he brought his team to Laramie.)

I met Bill Schrage in Laramie, Wyoming, to begin research. He introduced me to Vance Burch, Erin Wedemeyer, Danny Nelson, Rick Stuart, and Pat and Roger McMicheal. Bill and I headed to the American Heritage Center on the University of Wyoming campus to meet archivist John Waggener, who gave me a tour of the facility, focusing on the Kenny Sailors collection.

Bill drove me past homes where a young Kenny had lived. There were schools, gymnasiums, fields, university buildings, statues to see, and Wyoming hospitality to enjoy.

Rick Stuart escorted me around town, stopping to see the log home Kenny and Marilynne had built with the help of their Swedish craftsman friend. We took in the sights of apartments, parks, more statues, Greek houses at the UW, and the graves of Kenny and his mother Cora.

Vance Burch walked me through *Hell's Half Acre* and *the Union* buildings. The atmosphere, memorabilia, and rich history I was able to experience were valuable in describing incidents from Kenny's basketball career.

Erin Wedemeyer graciously shared her wonderful collection of Kenny memorabilia with me. We laughed as she showed off the photograph of Kenny and his stint as a prune juice promoter. Erin and her son Ethan had very special relationships with their uncle and great-uncle.

Pat and Roger McMicheal were gracious hosts to me on another trip I made. I heard more stories of this man who had made numerous contributions, not only in the world of basketball, but in the lives of countless people.

A chance encounter with Patrick Gabriel, a radio announcer at Wyoming Public Media, led to additional information and details that were helpful in the final preparation of Kenny's story. Much appreciated.

John Faulkner helped me wrap up the final details on the group of folks who had become Kenny's friends and supporters.

Dozens of hours were spent at the AHC utilizing the Sailors collection. The boxes of memorabilia contain newspaper and magazine articles, hard-copy photos, and correspondence as well as CDs, DVDs, and videos. The majority of the newspaper clippings were likely compiled by Kenny's mother Cora and wife Marilynne in the 1940s. The articles I perused rarely had newspaper names or bylines.

Dan Sailors was always willing to listen and sympathize when I was stuck. Then he cheered me on. I reconnected with friend Sandy McMahan of Gakona and e-met her husband Chuck, who was in the guiding business with Ken for twenty years. What great folks to collect information from and visit with.

Troy Reichert answered a phone call from an "unknown caller," yours truly, and brought the final chapter into focus. Coach Reichert and Brian Steiner brought this story to an exceptional close.

I'm mighty grateful for the input and encouragement each of these folks added to this project. Without their assistance, this book would not be possible.

Deb DeArmond, my writing coach, and editor Ann Tatlock were key to guiding me in creating this project.

Many thanks to my prayer partners: Andrew, Kerry, Lauryn, Ayla, Taylor S., Ben, Cerissa, Kane, Lilly, Max, Hugo, Gary, Jinx, Bruce, Peggy, Dedra, Tom, Suzanne, Sandi, Pat, Dave, Dan S., Bill, Rick, Maggie, Vance, Pat, Roger, Danny N., Linda, Dedra, Taylor J., Carrie J., Phoebe, Gabe, Cathy, Nancy, Marilyn, Bill, Deb D., Janay, Stacy, Betty, and those who are unnamed.

I want to encourage you to use what you have to make a difference in your world. Do your best. Move beyond where you are. Become a person of grit and gumption. Elevate your life to inspire others.

BIBLIOGRAPHY

BOOKS

Christgau, John. *The Origins of the JUMP SHOT – Eight Men Who Shook the World of Basketball:* University of Nebraska Press, 1999.

The Alaska Almanac. *Facts About Alaska.* Fifteenth Edition. Alaska Northwest Books. A division of GTE Discovery Publications, Inc. 22026 20th Avenue S.E. Bothell, Washington 98021. 1991

Freedman, Lew. *JUMP SHOT.* Kenny Sailors. Basketball Innovator and Alaskan Outfitter. WestWinds Press, Portland, Oregon. 2014.

Fury, Shawn. *Rise and Fire.* Flatiron Books, 175 Fifth Avenue, New York, NY 10010. 2016

Gilders, Michelle A. Gilders, Essays by. *Crossing Alaska.* Graphic Arts Center Publishing Company, P.O. Box 10306 Portland, OR 97296-0306. 1997.

HILLSDALE HERITAGE. Published by Hillsdale Homemakers Club. Printed by Pioneer Printing Company, PO Box 466, Cheyenne, Wyoming 82001. Copyright October 1976.

Sailors, Kenny and Freedman, Lew. *Hunting the Wild Country: Forty Years as a Guide in Alaska.* Glacier Press, Anchorage, Alaska, 1994.

the facts. Trans Alaska pipeline system. Booklet. Alyeska Pipeline Service Company, PO Box 196660, Anchorage, AK 99519-6660. Printed 2007.

Thorburn, Ryan. *COWBOY UP;* Kenny Sailors, The Jump Shot and Wyoming's Championship Basketball History. Burning Daylight an imprint of Pearn and Associates, Inc. 1600 Edora Court Suite D, Fort Collins, Colorado 80525. 2011.

NEWSPAPERS, MAGAZINES, AND ONLINE STORIES

Associated Press. *"Marines Trounce Dow Chemical."* Ogden Standard Examiner, March 8, 1944. http://www.newspapers.com/image/27101314.

Copper River Country Journal, March 3, 1994. Volume 8, Number 9. Printed by Northcountry Communications, Inc. POB 336, Glennallen, Alaska, 99588

denverpost.com. "*Wyoming's Sailors gave basketball a giant leap forward in the 1930s*". By Anthony Cotton. The Denver Post. Posted 03/21/2010.

Effrat, Louis. "18,316 See Wyoming Quintet Beat St. John's in Overtime." New York Times, April 2, 1943. http://query.nytimes.com/gst/abstract.html?res=9F05E2DB1730E53BBC4A53DFB2668388659EDE.

Kritzer, Cy. "Ken Sailors' Play Helps Wyoming to Sail to Cage Titles." *Sporting News,* April 8, 1943.

Marine Corps Chevron. "Marine Cagers Await USC Trojans." December 18, 1943. http://historicperiodicals.pinceton.edu/historic/

cgi-bin/historic?a=d&d=MarineCorpsChevron19431218-01.1.17&e=---en-20—1—txt-IN---#.

----. "In Search of a Lost Jump Shot." *New London Day,* June 3, 1985. https://news.google.com/newspapers?nid=1915&-dat=19850603&id=q5hGAAAAIBAJ&sjid=hvgMAAAAIBAJ&pg-2091,512217&hl=en.

Powers, Ian. "Kenny Sailors and the Jump Shot Heard 'Round the World." New York *Daily News*, March 23, 2014. http://creative.nydailynews.com/jumpshot.

The New York Times. https://www.nytimes.com/2016/01/31/sports/basketball/Kenny-sailors-a-pioneer-of-the-jump-shot-dies-at-95.html

Time magazine, "Cowboys v. Indians." Monday, April 12, 1943. Time Inc. 225 Liberty Street, New York City. en.m.wikipedia.org/wiki/Time_(magazine).

United Press. "San Diego Marine Cagers Have Won 20 Straight Tilts." *Nevada State Journal* (Reno), January 13, 1944. http//www.newspapers.com/image/75299215.

United Press. "San Diego Marines Trim Southern Cal." Tucson Daily Citizen, January 29, 1944. http://www.newspapers.com/image/9800289.

VIDEOS - DVDs & ORAL HISTORIES

Cowboys. The Story of the 1943 Wyoming Championship Basketball Team. Directed and produced by Kim Komenich. Written and Produced by G. Allen Johnson. Broad Ripple Films Productions 2014. American Heritage Center, University of Wyoming.

Jump Shot. The Kenny Sailors Story. DVD. Executive producer Stephen Curry. Director/Producer Jacob Hamilton. Aspiration Entertainment 2020.

NPR Story Corps, cd - Kenny Sailors with Anne Brande. July 3, 2008.

University of Wyoming Archives Kenny Sailors Collection. Audio files: 1-22. https://archiveswest.orbiscascade.org/ark:/80444/xv678186

University of Wyoming oral history of Kenny Sailors. http://digital-collections.uwyo.edu:8180/luna/servlet/uwydbuwy~91~91

Providence vs. Washington video. Box #6, Kenny Sailors, Collection #12537 American Heritage Center, University of Wyoming.

Wyoming Senator Joseph C. O'Mahoney interview. Box #6, 1959 DVD interview, Kenny Sailors Collection #12537 American Heritage Center, University of Wyoming.

Kenny Sailors. *Leap of Faith.* DVD. Wyoming PBS 2013. www.wyomingpbs.org American Heritage Center, University of Wyoming.

INTERVIEWS, E-MAILS, AND PHONE CALLS

Ken Brown, Vance Burch, Dave Dagenhart, Pat Dagenhart, John Faulkner, Carrie Gallegos, Kelly Gerlach, Jake Hamilton, Chuck McMahan, Sandy McMahan, Pat McMicheal, Roger McMicheal, Danny Nelson, Troy Reichert, Dale Sailors, Dan Sailors, Wendy Sailors, Bill Schrage, Brian Steiner, Rick Stuart, Denise Major Wallace, Erin Wedemeyer, John R. Waggener.

APPENDIX

KENNY SAILORS – BASKETBALL HONORS

1934	-Inventor of the modern-day jump shot
1941-42	-All-Skyline Conference selection
1942-43	-Captain of Wyoming Cowboys basketball team that finished 31-2
	-Most Valuable Player NCAA championships, leading Wyoming to the title
	-All-Skyline Conference selection
1943	-Winner Chuck Taylor Award as best college player in the United States
	-College All-American
	-Amateur Athletic Union All-American
1945-46	-All-Skyline Conference selection
	-College All-American
	-Winner Helms Foundation Award as best college player in the United States
1946-47	-Member Cleveland Rebels, NBA

1947-48	-Member Chicago Stages/Philadelphia Warriors/ Providence Steamrollers, NBA
1948-49	-Member Providence Steamrollers, NBA
1949-50	-Member Denver Nuggets, NBA
1950-51	-Member Boston Celtics/Baltimore Bullets, NBA
1990	-Honored as NCAA Final Four as NCAA tournament player of the 1940s
1993	-Inducted as member of first class, University of Wyoming Intercollegiate Athletics Hall of Fame
2005	-Chosen as a member of University of Wyoming All-Century Team
2008	-Received the prestigious University of Wyoming Medallion Service Award; the number 4 playing jersey retired by UW
2012	-Inducted into College Basketball Hall of Fame -Selected as one of the best 75 NCAA tournament players of all time
2017	-Statue of Kenny shooting his famous jump shot unveiled in the UW Arena-Auditorium
2024	-To be inducted into the American Basketball Hall of Fame Class

ABOUT THE AUTHOR

Debbie Sorensen has written articles for newspapers and magazines from the East Coast to the West Coast of the US. She continues to write bi-monthly reports for a national fraternal organization. This is her first book, inspired by the story of a friend Kenny, who chose to overcome and elevate his purpose in life.

Basketball has been a part of Debbie's life for decades: first following two sons in the sport and now cheering on six basketball playing grandchildren. She loves to encourage countless other young hoopsters by sharing the story of how one person made a difference. Debbie can be reached through her website: www.welcoming-words.com